OCR

Revise

Geography

OCR and Hei~~~~~ ~~~~~ ~~~~~ support for you

Chris Martin

OCR
RECOGNISING ACHIEVEMENT

Heinemann

Official Publisher Partnership

Heinemann is an imprint of Pearson Education Limited, a company incorporated in England and Wales, having its registered office at Edinburgh Gate, Harlow, Essex, CM20 2JE. Registered company number: 872828

www.heinemann.co.uk

Heinemann is a registered trademark of Pearson Education Limited

Text © Pearson Education Limited 2009

First published 2009

13 12 11 10 09
10 9 8 7 6 5 4 3 2

British Library Cataloguing in Publication Data
A catalogue record for this book is available from the British Library.

ISBN 978 0 435357 70 2

Copyright notice

Edited by Lucy Hyde
Designed by Wooden Ark Studio
Typeset by Phoenix Photosetting, Chatham, Kent
Original illustrations © Pearson Education Limited 2009
Illustrated by Phoenix Photosetting
Cover design by Pearson Education
Cover photo/illustration © Bernhard Edmaier
Printed in Malaysia, CTP-PJB

Acknowledgements
Every effort has been made to contact copyright holders of material reproduced in this book. Any omissions will be rectified in subsequent printings if notice is given to the publishers.

Contents

Introduction

This book is designed to aid your AS Geography revision. It is specifically aimed at the OCR specification but much of it is still relevant to other AS specifications – especially AQA. It seeks to provide the basic points you need to cover in each topic. It is assumed that you will fill in the detail from what you have been taught or from the Heinneman student book written to support the specification, and this is referred to in the text to steer you to the relevant pages. Much of the material is an enlarged version of the 'refresh your memory' sections in the student book and student support CD but there are some additional case studies. The revision tips and other advice is drawn partly from the student book and is a shortened version containing the most important elements.

Revision tips

So how do you learn all the material that you need for the examination?

What learning style are you?

Firstly you need to discover your preferred learning style. Which of the following do you find is the easiest way to learn and recall information?

Learning style	Revision aids
Visual	Draw maps and diagrams Spider diagrams Use headings Use mnemonics Use CD-ROM or Internet
Auditory	Record someone reading your notes Make up rhymes or songs Get someone to quiz you
Kinesthetic	Cut up sections of notes and rearrange them Build models of things Act out aspects Card indexes

Most geographers are visual learners; hence the two most-used aids to memory and revision are:

1) Mnemonics

This where a word or phrase is used to recall a list of information. Throughout the textbook a number of these have been used to help your revision:

◆ PESP = geographical factors = Physical, Economic, Social and Political

◆ CRDVDS = physical or environmental factors = Climate, Relief, Drainage, Vegetation, Disease and wildlife, Soils and geology

◆ SPITMAS = human factors = Settlement, Power, Industry, Transport, Mining and quarrying, Agriculture, Services

2) Spider diagrams

These are ideal as essay plans as they show the interconnections and logic of geographical factors and features.

Timing

Remember that some people can revise more easily at certain times of the day. Know when you learn best. Also take regular breaks – take a 10- to 15-minute break in every hour and don't revise all day. Revise in manageable chunks or topics. You will need to go over it several times before it sticks in your long-term memory.

The specification

If you haven't got a copy check it out on the OCR website.

At AS level there are two papers – Physical and Human. You are required to study all four units for each of the papers **but** you only have to answer questions on three of them.

Of the four units, two are existing topics probably studied earlier in your time in school and two are relatively new topics. The new ones tend to have less content as it is assumed you have not studied them before, so you may need to take longer to assimilate the content.

	Physical	Human
Well known	Rivers Coasts	Urban Rural
Relatively new	Cold (glacial) Hot arid (desert)	Tourism Energy

The content is set out under three headings:

Questions for investigation – these set the broad context and pose questions that could be answered by research and fieldwork.

Key ideas – these set out some of the approaches that could be used to answer the question.

Content – this gives a minimum list of topics and concepts that you can be expected to cover in the time available. You can go beyond this but you should not try to leave any of this out. Questions will often use wording from this section.

Each topic has four questions to investigate. Each question increases in complexity and becomes more debatable. So the first section is usually quite factual and is related to patterns and processes. By section four, it is more applied, focusing on efforts to make the system more manageable or sustainable.

Case studies and examples

Throughout the examination you are expected to refer to real places and locations in your answer. If the question asks for named examples it means locations. The specification sets out the minimum number of examples or case studies needed to illustrate a particular topic. These should be contrasts in some aspects which then allows you to compare.

These are examples of the key idea(s); **not** case studies as such. There should be enough detail to show a knowledge and understanding of the location

but not too much that it gets in the way of what it is exemplifying. Sketching maps to show locations can be useful but sometimes they just distract and waste your time.

The local small-scale example from your own area or knowledge is often quite powerful and examiners like to see examples that go beyond the student book ones.

Assessment objectives

The exam paper has been set out to match the assessment objectives:

AO1 – Knowledge and understanding account for 50 per cent of the marks and these are usually assessed in sections a, b and c of a question. These require you to know concepts, processes, facts and locations.

AO2 – Analyse, interpret and evaluate issues and apply understanding. This is basically about cause–effect relationships. This is worth 20 per cent and tends to be assessed in section d and the essay.

AO3 – Investigate, conclude and communicate – rather a mixed objective but it includes geographical skills and techniques and the ability to communicate effectively the conclusions of an investigation. This is worth 30 per cent and is again most likely in section d and the essay.

The examination

Both papers are similar in design and layout. They are both 1 hour 30 minutes long and are marked out of 75, of which each question is marked out of 25.

Remember:

1) **You can't answer the essay in section B from the same topic you answered in section A**

2) **You must choose in section A – you have to do one well-known topic (e.g. rivers or coasts) and one relatively new topic (e.g. cold or hot arid)**

It is probably best to read the essay titles first and decide which one you would like to do. This will influence your choice in section A.

Do the section A questions first as the time left will influence your depth and style of essay. Remember it's about a minute a mark so a six-mark question should take six minutes maximum. The lines on the question paper suggest the length of your answer but you can use the extra pages at the back of the booklet if you find you need more space.

Question wording – command words

These are vital as they direct your approach. You must know what they mean and what they are asking you to do.

One of the commonest errors candidates make is in not understanding what the question is asking. The understanding of the meaning of terms used in questions is crucial in appreciating what the question and examiner want. A lot of time and trouble go into deciding the exact phrasing of a question so every word is vital. Some terms are regularly misunderstood. Terms that are typically used at AS level include:

Comment Present an informed opinion. (Back up an opinion with examples, evidence.)

Compare Identify similarities, supported with evidence.

Contrast Identify differences, supported with evidence.

Describe Set out its characteristics or appearance – a diagram or map may be helpful.

Examine Investigate closely. (Describe, explain and comment on…)

Explain Set out purposes, reasons or causes: why is it like that, why is it there, why does it happen that way? (Think physical and/or human factors.)

Identify Name or otherwise characterise (refer to direction or location in a photograph or quote grid references from a map).

Illustrate Present clarifying or explaining examples.

Outline Briefly set out main characteristics.

Summarise Make a summary of; expressing concisely.

State Express in unequivocal terms. (Simple factual response expected – often a figure or a name.)

Suggest Put forward appropriate possibilities giving sensible reasons (you are not expected to know the exact ones).

Show Indicate or explain.

Discuss Consider by debating a topic or issue: present the points for and against.

Question types

These each require a different approach.

1) Data response (section a or a i)

This is usually the first part of a question worth 4 marks and is designed to see if you can interpret (read the implications of) a diagram. Sometimes you are expected to describe the trend or state the values of something. This you do by reading off the diagram the values using the key or scale on the axes. You must quote real values. Saying 'it's high' isn't good enough. Trends can be positive or negative, strong or weak. Always look for odd values (anomalies) that don't fit in. In other cases you are asked to compare or describe the relationship between two or more variables. In this case you **must not** describe one then the other but write in sentences that combine both variables. Again, relationships can be positive or negative, linear or non-linear and strong or weak.

Often you are asked to describe patterns. Saying where something isn't is as important as where it is. Use compass points and the scale to identify aspects of patterns. You might want to refer to the shape of the pattern – linear, circular, amorphous, etc.

You may be asked to identify features shown in a photograph. Often these are numbered or lettered. Examiners do recognise that there may be more than one interpretation of the indicated features. If there are no letters then sometimes a quick sketch helps; if not then use terms like 'top-right' to indicate features.

This is the stage at which you may be expected to read data off an OS map. Don't forget how to do six figure grid references. When the question asks you to refer to the map it wants references and place names.

2) Short answers

These are worth six marks and normally ask you to explain, outline or suggest something related to the data response. These questions test your knowledge and understanding, e.g. how landforms are created. These questions do not require more than two points but they should be developed in depth and if you can give a located example then do so. **Remember: depth is more important than a lot of superficial points.** This is where your mnemonics come in useful. Remember that you can use appropriate diagrams to help your answer and they can reduce the amount you have to write, e.g. it is difficult and long winded to describe a glacial hanging valley. These questions are marked on two levels – the higher one (5–6 marks) expects clear cause/effect and the correct use of geographical terms.

3) Extended answers

These are worth nine marks and are in effect mini-essays without introductions and conclusions. It is worth reading these sections before finalising your choice of questions. They mostly draw on the later sections of each topic and you will often see that they use the wording in the specification. You are expected to use your located examples to illustrate your argument.

4) Essays

These are worth a third of the marks for the paper and are designed to distinguish those candidates that can analyse questions and construct effective arguments. There is space on the paper for you to plan your answer. Remember: if you do run out of time to finish your answer then this plan will be looked at to see where you had intended to go. Planning is important to structure your answer. Each paragraph should have a distinctive grouping of ideas, e.g. physical, economic and social.

Crucial to your essay is your introduction, which shows your understanding of the question, the line of argument you will follow and the examples you are using to support this argument. Equally, if not more, important is your conclusion. This summarises your argument and draws together what has gone before to conclude – agreeing or disagreeing with the initial question is less important than saying the chief reasons why. Do remember there is rarely a totally definitive answer. It usually depends on where you are (e.g. rural versus urban, coastal versus inland, MEDC versus LEDC) and the group's viewpoint (e.g. rich versus poor, young versus old, single versus family).

Try to understand the paper

Always get hold of past papers and use them to find out how the examiner words the questions. You can use these to practise your ability to read and answer questions within the time allocated. **(But beware – there is a risk you will put in your answer what you hope the examiner is asking or what they asked previously.)** You can also look for patterns of questions. All exam papers are set using a specification grid to help avoid duplication or repetition. January and June examinations are set at the same time – usually two years in advance. What was in the news then? Even better, get hold of the examiner's report, on the exam board website or from your teacher, as this contains helpful advice on how to improve performance paper by paper and question by question.

The layout of this revision guide

This revision guide follows the headings and content in the OCR specification and the Heinneman student book, but it also includes some new content to enhance case study material.

Key words

These are some of the geographical terms that you can be expected to know and use. They are defined in the student book.

Diagrams

There are diagrams included for the physical topics. These are not meant to be definitive but rather the standard expected in the examination in limited time to illustrate the formation and appearance of key landforms.

Quick check questions

These are designed to allow you to test your knowledge of some of the revision points at the end of each section. These are not the factual types of questions you can expect in the examination.

Exam tips

These are helpful suggestions relevant to the OCR examination but are not hints about actual questions as such.

Exam Café

These occur at the end of each chapter and are based on the style of questions you can expect in the examination. To save space, the diagrams referred to in the questions have not been included but their appearance is clear from the comments.

Processes at work in river basins

Weathering

> **Student book pages 9–11**

Weathering is the disintegration and decomposition of rocks in situ. There are several types:

Mechanical – no change in state; just disintegrates. Usually occurs as a result of pressure changes in the rock, such as:

- freeze-thaw – water expands 9 per cent when it freezes to form ice
- salt crystal growth – as crystals grow they exert pressure
- exfoliation – surface layer flakes off
- wet/dry – expands when wet and contracts when dry (e.g. mud)
- granular disintegration – rock crystals expand and contract
- block disintegration – jointed rocks expand and contract
- pressure release – weight is taken off the rock.

Chemical – change in state; just decomposes or rots. For example:

- Oxidation – oxygen reacts with minerals like iron (rusts)
- Carbonic acid – rainwater is weak carbonic acid
- Hydrolysis
- Hydration.

Biological – by plants and animals involving both mechanical impacts, such as root growth, and chemical impacts, such as the release of organic acids.

Mechanical weathering – roots exert pressure

Chemical weathering – organic acids dissolve, e.g. humic

Factors controlling the type and rate of weathering:

- Climate – heat speeds chemical up, cold favours freeze-thaw, temperature range favours mechanical. Moisture is crucial.
- Rock type – porosity, chemical composition, crystal make-up, hardness.
- Rock structure – beds, joints, faults.
- Vegetation – trees do more mechanical weathering than grass but grass holds moisture and organic acids.
- Drainage – dry areas suffer less chemical weathering.
- Aspect – the direction the sun or rain comes from is crucial.
- Rate of erosion – exposes fresh surfaces for weathering.
- Human activity – e.g. pollution causes acid rain.

Mass movement

> **Student book pages 6–8**

Mass movement is the movement of material under the force of gravity. It tends to reduce the slope angle.

Types of mass movement are usually classified on speed and water content:

- Slow – creep
- Fast – flows (wet), slides, slumps
- Very fast – avalanche, free fall.

Key words

Sheer resistance	Stability slope
Sheer strength	

Remember

Mass movement occurs due to a reduction in the sheer strength of the slope and/or an increase in sheer stress.

Factors controlling type and rate of movement:

◆ Climate – rain increases weight and lubricates

◆ Rock type – soft rocks flow and slide more, e.g. clay

◆ Rock structure – slope of beds is crucial

◆ Relief – steep slopes mean more movement

◆ Vegetation – tree roots reduce movement but can cause creep

◆ Drainage – dry areas suffer less movement

◆ Aspect – direction of rain is crucial

◆ Rate of erosion – removes already mass moved material so exposing the slope foot

◆ Shock from something to trigger it – e.g. traffic

◆ Human activity – making slopes steeper than their stability slope, e.g. cuttings.

Erosion

Erosion could be from wind, ice, sea, human activity or the river itself. The rate is determined by the energy available and the resistance of the surface. Storms and floods increase the rate of erosion.

Types of river erosion:

◆ Abrasion – load is used to wear away banks/bed

◆ Hydraulic – sheer force and weight of falling water

◆ Attrition – load collides and grinds away

◆ Solution – removal of chemical ions.

Transport

Transport could be by wind, ice, sea, human activity or the river itself. The rate is determined by the energy available and the weight of the load. The greater the energy and finer the load, the more can be carried.

Types of river transport:

◆ Floatation – on the surface

◆ Traction – rolling along the bed

◆ Saltation – bouncing along the bed

◆ Solution – dissolved in the water

◆ Suspension – held in the water.

Key words

Hydraulic	Traction
Attrition	Entrainment

Student book pages 15–16. Look at the section on the Hjulstrom curve. This can be used to help answers on river transport.

Deposition

Deposition could be from wind, ice, sea, human activity or the river itself. The rate is determined by the energy loss level and the weight of the load. A shallow gradient, a wider channel, a dryer climate or meeting the sea will slow the river.

The coarsest river deposits are deposited first as energy falls.

Types of river deposits:

◆ Bed load – coarse and dropped first. Cobbles, then pebbles, then sand

◆ Suspension – silt and sand

◆ Solution – rarely dropped unless mixes with salt in the estuary/delta.

Exam tips

Don't forget that using your fieldwork examples in your answer will impress the examiner.

Quick check questions

1 How much does water expand when it freezes?

2 Which type of weathering results in a change of state?

3 Which type of weathering would produce sand-sized particles?

4 Arrange the following in order of a) speed of movement and b) water content.

Creep, avalanche, flow, slide, free fall

5 What is a stability slope?

Factors responsible for fluvial processes and landforms

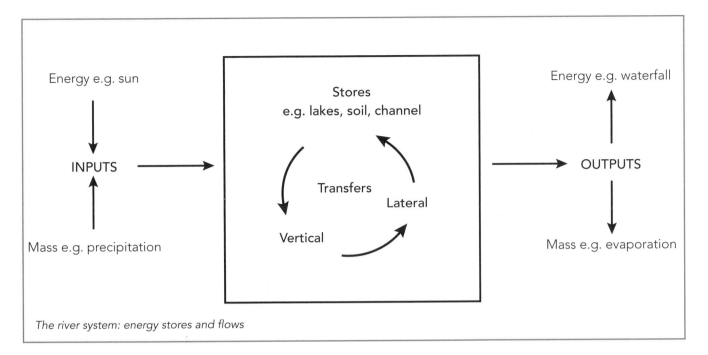

The river system: energy stores and flows

Channel factors

Channel factors control the energy and flow of the river. They include:

◆ Channel shape – a smaller wetted perimeter per cross-sectional area is more efficient (hydraulic radius)

◆ Channel size – larger channels are more efficient

◆ Roughness – the rougher the bed the lower the energy

◆ Gradient – a flatter gradient creates lower energy

◆ Load – a heavy load means little spare energy

◆ Base level – rising base level (usually the sea) means less energy

◆ Type of flow – turbulent flow uses energy

◆ Hydrograph – flashy hydrographs (sudden rise in flow) mean more energy.

Basin factors

Basin factors control the rate of inputs and stores. They include:

◆ Hydrological cycle/system – size of stores in the system

◆ Size of basin – larger basins are slower to react

◆ Shape of basin – narrow long basins react more slowly

◆ River network – complex networks slow the flow

◆ River density – denser systems slow the flow.

Key words

Hydraulic radius	Turbulent flow
Efficiency	Wetted perimeter
Discharge	

Exam tips

Although hydrographs are not mentioned in the specification they are useful when comparing river regimes.

Other factors

Other factors control flows and stores, inputs and outputs. These include the factors listed below.

Physical factors:

◆ Climate – precipitation type/volume, evaporation, temperature

◆ Relief – slope, altitude, base level

◆ Rock type – geology, structure (faults, beds, porosity, tilt of rocks)

◆ Soil – permeability, thickness, organic content

◆ Vegetation – type and percentage cover.

Human factors:

◆ Water supply – abstraction

◆ Channel work – dams, weirs, embankments, straightening, widening, deepening, dredging, flood prevention, meander management

◆ Drainage – of soils, from industries, roads, etc

◆ Agriculture – crop type, deforestation, irrigation, drainage

◆ Urbanisation – impervious surfaces, channel controls

◆ Transport – canalisation, bridges, weirs.

Time factors:

◆ Previous weather

◆ Climatic change

◆ Tectonic changes.

Quick check questions

1 Which is more efficient: a) a 25 metre wide, 5 metre deep or b) a 5 metre wide, 1 metre deep channel? Explain your answer.

2 Why is 'base level' so called?

3 What could create a 'local base level'?

4 State three stores in river basin systems.

5 Why might agriculture a) increase runoff into rivers b) decrease it?

Exam tips

This is the type of diagram examiners would expect. Any more detail and you would waste time.

River features

Student book pages 17–22

You should be able to **describe** river features, i.e. their shape, size, location, composition, and **explain** how they were formed. The most effective way is to use well-annotated diagrams.

Exam tips

Don't use colours on your diagrams as they will be scanned as black and white for marking online.

Most questions ask you to describe and explain two features of erosion and deposition:

Deposition features

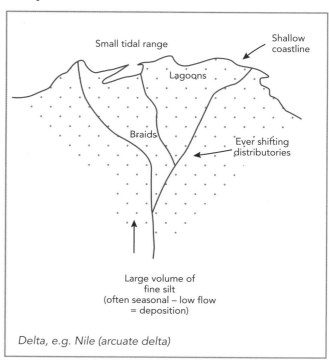

Small tidal range

Shallow coastline

Lagoons

Braids

Ever shifting distributories

Large volume of fine silt
(often seasonal – low flow = deposition)

Delta, e.g. Nile (arcuate delta)

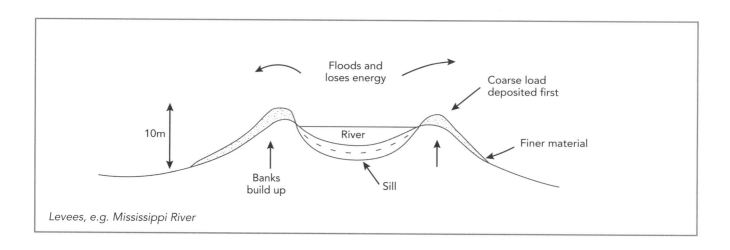

Floods and loses energy

Coarse load deposited first

10m

River

Finer material

Banks build up

Sill

Levees, e.g. Mississippi River

Erosion features

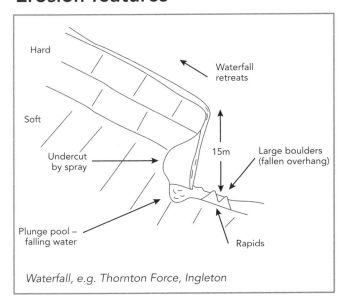

Hard

Soft

Waterfall retreats

15m

Large boulders (fallen overhang)

Undercut by spray

Plunge pool – falling water

Rapids

Waterfall, e.g. Thornton Force, Ingleton

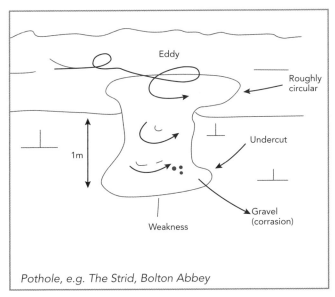

Eddy

Roughly circular

Undercut

1m

Weakness

Gravel (corrasion)

Pothole, e.g. The Strid, Bolton Abbey

Quick check questions

1 Why are meanders features of river erosion and deposition?

2 Why do meanders move downstream?

3 What two features does a pothole need to form in a river bed?

4 Why are levees dangerous?

5 Why are 'bird's foot deltas' rare?

River basins as multi-use resources

Uses of river basins include:

◆ Power – water mills, hydro-electric (green energy as clean and renewable)

◆ Industry – fishing, flat land ideal for heavy industry, etc

◆ Water supply – groundwater (acquifer), reservoirs, water transfer schemes

◆ Settlement – flat land, pleasant views, water supply

◆ Services – tourism, recreation, waste disposal

◆ Minerals – sediments (e.g. gravel/sand), oil/gas, placer deposits (e.g. tin)

◆ Agriculture – irrigation, drainage, fertile silts, fish farms

◆ Transport – ports, bulk cargoes

◆ Conservation – river meadows, marshlands, nature reserves.

Conflicts between land uses

Conflicts may be because one activity impacts on another (e.g. wildlife is disturbed by motorboats), activities compete to use the same water (e.g. irrigation versus drinking water) or an activity changes the nature of the water for another user (e.g. industrial water pollution on drinking water). Other conflicts arise as water is a fluid so moves from one area to another with its contents (e.g. fish).

Conflicts can be:

◆ between different land uses/activities, e.g. Mekong – Dams threaten fishing, transport and farming

or:

◆ within the same land use/activity, e.g. Thames – recreation in the estuary sees conflicts between wind surfers, swimmers, power boats, sailing, jet skis and fishing.

Case study: rivers as multi-use resources

Student book pages 23–30

	Thames MEDC *Covers 13,000 km² and has a population of 12 million* *Very uniform flow – estuary*	Mekong LEDC/NIC *Covers 800,000 km² and has a population of 55 million* *Seasonal with monsoons – delta*
Power	Old water mills but no HEP	Increasing dam construction. First one 1993 in China. Only 5% of potential used
Industry	Bulky industries like oil refining, cement, paper along the estuary and Thames Corridor of hi-tech industry	Major fishing area – 2 million tonnes. 1200 different species. Newly industrialising area – heavy industry
Water supply	Supplies 5000 million litres a day much from groundwater	Supplies the bulk of water to 55 million people
Settlement	London, Oxford, Reading and planned Thames Gateway development	High population but high flood risk
Services	Recreation and leisure, e.g. cruising, fishing, sailing at Cotswold Water Park	Rapid growth as tourist area
Minerals	Sand and gravel around Reading	Sand, gravel. Potential for placer deposits and gas in delta
Agriculture	Arable farming – some use of irrigation for market gardening	80% of rice production depends on water and river silt
Transport	London still a port and Tilbury. Limited barge traffic up the Thames	Barges to Phnom Penh but dry season produces sand bars
Conservation	Thames estuary mudflats, e.g. Benfleet marshes	None as yet
Waste disposal	Waste sewage is dumped off the estuary mouth and a number of landfill sites, e.g. Pitsea	Most sewage and industrial waste is dumped in the river

Case study: conflicts in the Thames Estuary (shown by X)

Conflicts	Fishing e.g. shellfish	Waste disposal e.g. sewage	Tourism e.g. swimming	Recreation e.g. sailing	Shipping e.g. containers	Industry e.g. oil refining	Sand/ gravel
Fishing		X	X	X	X	X	X
Waste disposal	X		X	X	X		X
Tourism	X	X		X	X	X	X
Recreation	X	X	X	X	X	X	X
Shipping	X	X	X	X	X		X
Industry	X		X	X			
Sand/gravel	X	X	X	X	X		

Flooding

Causes of river flooding

◆ Sudden intense heavy rainfall, e.g. Worcestershire and Gloucestershire 2007

◆ Prolonged heavy rain, e.g. Lynton and Lynmouth 1952 (heavy rain for 12 days out of 14 in August)

◆ Sudden seasonal snow melt, e.g. UK following heavy snow in 1947

◆ Rapid runoff in a small basin, e.g. Boscastle in August 2004

◆ Steep slopes cause rapid runoff

◆ Deforestation so reducing interception and increasing runoff etc, e.g. Bangladesh in 2007

◆ Increased impermeable surfaces following urbanisation, e.g. Gloucester in 2007

◆ Dam bursting, e.g. the Vaiont Dam in Italy 1963 killed 3000

Case study: Bangladesh versus Gloucester – causes of flooding

	Severn and Avon – Gloucester, 2007	Ganges and Bramaputra – Bangladesh, 2007
Natural factors	River rose 6m above normal	
Climate	Prolonged heavy rain – 320% more than average	Heavy monsoon rains and global warming melting snow in the Himalayas
Relief	Wide flat floodplain	Over 50% of area less than 5m above sea level. 75% of population live in the delta. Area is sinking due to water abstraction.
Drainage	Severn and Avon – both in flood – meet above Gloucester	Three major rivers meet in the delta. Rivers high in load so frequently deposit
Vegetation	Little woodland – mostly farmed area	Deforestation in Himalayas (source of rivers)
Geology	Largely impervious Triassic clays	Largely impervious silts and clays
Human factors		
Urbanisation	Increasingly being built up, especially on the floodplain. Increased impervious surfaces	Very dense population and rapidly growing (2.7%)
Farming	Intensive arable – use of heavy machinery compacts soil	Intensive rice cultivation – relies on floods but created waterlogged fields
Transport	Numerous bridges and 'ponded' water, e.g. Evesham	Relatively few bridges as rivers frequently change course or braid
River controls	Minimal but use of weirs and locks on Avon. Some channel controls on the Severn, e.g. Shrewsbury	Few in Bangladesh as so big and few funds but India does embank and divert so speeding the flow

◆ High tide or storm surge backing up water in rivers, e.g. east coast of England in 1953 and 1978

◆ Geophysical events, e.g. flooding following Mt St Helen's eruption in 1980.

Impact of flooding

This may be immediate (e.g. rescuing those people stranded), medium term (e.g. damage to property) or longer term (e.g. damage to house prices).

Case study: Bangladesh versus Gloucester – impacts of flooding

	Severn and Avon – Gloucester, 2007	Ganges and Bramaputra – Bangladesh, 2007
Casualties	Few – 3	Over 300 – 35 from snakebites
Disease	None	Lots of fever and diarrhoea
Property	1350 properties flooded in Gloucester city; 500 elsewhere	300,000 moved to refugee camps. More than 7 million had some property damage
Pollution	Sewage contamination and engine oil from flooded cars	Drinking water contaminated with sewage
Services	350,000 homes lost their water supply. 48,000 homes lost power supply	Schools and clinics destroyed
Environment	Destruction of marshland habitats	Destruction of wetlands and protective coastal mangrove swamps
Farming	Top soil removed, animals drowned, crops lost	600,000 hectares flooded, loss of crops and animals
Economy	Shops and factories flooded, e.g. Barbourne	Shrimp and fishing industries badly hit. Factories destroyed
Transport	Several bridges washed away and roads blocked, e.g. M5, or swept away isolating villages, e.g. Fladbury	10,000km of road submerged and 80 bridges destroyed
Cost	£3 billion – only some covered by insurance	Impossible to estimate but in excess of $60 billion

Key words

Bankfull	Floodplain
Flashy hydrograph	Terraces

Flood prevention

Reasons for preventing floods – apply these to an area:

◆ Protect population

◆ Protect property and farmland

◆ Safeguard transport

◆ Avoid costs of floods

◆ Stop problems elsewhere

◆ Protect infrastructure, e.g. transport, power stations

◆ Conservation (historical and biotic)

◆ Create jobs.

But remember: prevention may impact elsewhere. Consider the costs versus benefits – is it worth the cost?

Methods of prevention

1. Hard engineering:

◆ Dams and reservoirs – store water

◆ Channel enlargement – dredging it wider and/or deeper

◆ Embankments or levees (or temporary flood walls)

◆ Flood relief channels – funnel water away

◆ Shorten river courses – cut off meanders

◆ Wing dykes – act like groynes and direct water away from banks

◆ Holding basins – to store floodwater in

◆ Barriers or barrages, e.g. Thames barrier.

2. Soft engineering:

◆ Marshland – naturally holds and stores water

◆ Afforestation (especially in upper catchment areas).

3. Planning restrictions:

◆ Farming controls – e.g. contour ploughing to reduce runoff

◆ Limits on urbanisation – reduce building on floodplains

◆ Insist on rainwater harvesting by new buildings, e.g. Germany.

4. Planned retreat:

◆ Flood proofing – e.g. buildings with lower floors, electrics etc designed to cope with a flood

◆ Design buildings to float with floods, e.g. Netherlands

◆ Flood basins – areas allowed to flood to reduce pressure on river channel.

5. Behavioural:

◆ Flood forecasting – so can prepare and people know the risks

◆ Flood warnings and evacuation strategies

◆ Insurance.

6. Do nothing:

◆ Evacuation and emergency planning.

Where should these measures occur?

◆ floodplain

◆ channel

◆ upper catchment

◆ entire basin

◆ channel/valley sides.

Schemes can be large scale (e.g. the Mississippi) or can be quite local (e.g Prittlebrook, Southend – an urban stream).

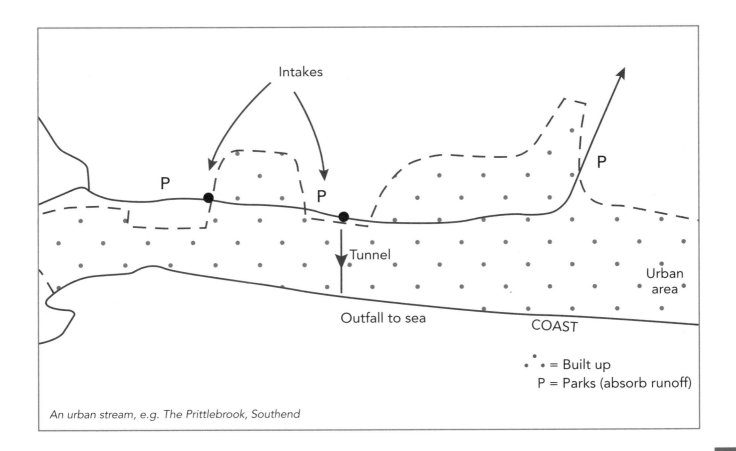

Intakes

P

P

Tunnel

P

Urban area

Outfall to sea

COAST

• • • = Built up
P = Parks (absorb runoff)

An urban stream, e.g. The Prittlebrook, Southend

Quick check questions

1 When do most flash floods occur in the UK and why?

2 Why are there few, if any, geophysical floods in the UK?

3 Why is Bangladesh so flood prone?

4 Why are there few river control systems in LEDCs?

5 What is the difference between hard and soft engineering?

Exam tips

Remember, management will depend on the nature of the river, scale, technology, capital available, likelihood of event, perception and costs/benefits.

Management challenges

Management challenges involve balancing the environmental needs (e.g. wildlife, hydrology, vegetation) against economic factors (e.g. farming, employment, transport) and social factors (e.g. people's sense of safety, security of property, pleasant scenery, historic/cultural aspects).

Issues:

◆ What is the exact nature of the water resources and their status (quality versus quantity)? We lack data on most river basins.

◆ Sheer cost – short versus long term, e.g. Thames Flood barrage cost £500 million in 1980. Who should pay? Local versus national issue – rate payer (or water board) versus tax payer.

◆ Who pays versus who gains? Should tax payers subsidise developments that benefit a small group, e.g. farmers? The death of the Aral Sea exemplifies this. How effective is the scheme and for whom?

◆ Political will, e.g. Rhine flows through four countries. Notion of Riparian states – the power that countries near the source have over those further down, e.g. India and Bangladesh.

- Ownership – who is responsible for the river? How far do their rights extend in the river basin?
- Technology – has the area the knowledge and expertise to develop the basin? Is enough known about that particular river and its basin?
- Size or scale – definition of the area that makes up the basin. It is easier to manage smaller areas, e.g. the Mississippi drains one-fifth of the USA.
- How long it will take – quick fix versus long term, e.g. Thames barrage will not cope with the forecast rise in the sea level.
- Wider impacts. What implications are there for areas beyond the basin, e.g. coastal or estuarine areas, and for other non-hydrological systems, e.g. climate?

Types of planning in river basins

Case study: basin management in England and Wales

This was in part a reaction by The Environmental Agency to drought problems but also flood control following the 2007 floods and the threat of global warming.

In 2008 DEFRA identified water bodies and divided the country into planning units – called River Basin Districts – based on river catchment areas. These areas were then characterised by assessing the pressures and impacts on the water environment, such as pollution or overuse.

Districts are expected to look at all water issues in their basins including:

- mapping water bodies and their ecosystems
- locating groundwater bodies
- identifying the impact human activities have on surface and groundwater
- devising strategies to protect and enhance water resources
- managing flood risks.

Each district is required to draw up a River Basin Management Plan which looks at integrating and co-ordinating the planning process. They are required to analyse costs and benefits to different sectors of implementing any proposals and involve the community in decision making.

Regional River Park, e.g. Lee Valley Leisure Park in East London

This is an example of managing a river for recreational activities. The total area is 4000 hectares and covers 37km of the river Lea including 100 lakes (mostly old gravel pits from the 1930s). The river was used for barges (so has locks and tow paths) and has flood diversion channels.

It was set up in 1966 as a Regional Park Authority to tidy up an area of gravel pits and derelict farming, and provide a much needed recreation space for the East End.

The area now attracts 3 million visitors for water sports and 10 million to the open spaces including a Country Park. There are numerous cycle paths, bridlepaths and walkways.

Although this landscape is less than a hundred years old, the flooded gravel pits and grassland are vital for birds and insects so much of the area has been designated a Site of Special Scientific Interest (SSSI) with several RSPB reserves.

Multi-purpose river scheme, e.g. Three Gorges Dam, Yangtze, China

This is a multi-purpose scheme to offset the massive cost ($30 billion) and act as a growth pole away from the rapidly developing coastal areas.

This dam was started in 1994 and opened in 2006 but is expected to be fully operational in 2011. It is located in the Xilingxia Gorge. The Yangtze drains 1 million km^2.

Purposes and advantages:

◆ Power – originally 10 per cent of China's total power need (now 3 per cent due to rapid growth). Largest Hydro station producing 22,500 MW from 34 generators. Power to nine provinces and cities such as Shanghai.

◆ Flood control. Will create a 560 km reservoir for storage. It will protect 15m people and 1.5m hectares of farmland. In the 1998 flood 1526 died and 2000 km^2 were flooded.

◆ Navigation. Five paired locks and a ship lift will increase river traffic five times to 5m tonnes and allow 10,000 barges to go 660km further upstream. Greatly reduces shipping costs.

◆ Water supply – reliable supply from the reservoir for irrigation, domestic and industrial uses especially in Shanghai.

◆ Environmental – clean renewable energy, reduces disease in the river, improves the micro-climate.

◆ Employment – creates numerous jobs and sets off a multiplier effect so generating development in this interior region.

◆ Fishing – new source in the new reservoir.

Disadvantages:

◆ Will flood 632km^2 and 25,00 hectares of farmland.

◆ Homes of nearly 1 million people will be flooded and 2.3 million will be forced to relocate.

◆ 1300 archaeological sites will be flooded.

◆ Silt will be trapped – damage to dam, turbines and loss of fertile silt below the dam. May impact on Yangtze delta and cause Shanghai to sink.

◆ Wildlife will be wiped out, e.g. Yangtze dolphin.

◆ Fishing and irrigation below the dam may be affected.

◆ It may be on a fault and the extra weight may set it off.

◆ It is vulnerable to attack.

Exam**Café**

Sample questions

(a) *Outline the ways in which a river carries its load. [4 marks]*

▶▶ See page 2.

- ◆ 'Outline' means there is no need to describe in detail.
- ◆ 'Outline' does not require you to explain.
- ◆ Four marks usually means there are at least four methods (there are) or means do two in detail.
- ◆ An annotated diagram would help to show where these 'ways' operate, e.g. traction along the river bed.

(b) *Explain why rivers may deposit their loads. [6 marks]*

▶▶ See page 2.

- ◆ Six marks normally require at least two reasons. In reality there is only one here – a loss of carrying capacity. This could be due to loss of energy (e.g. meets the sea, flatter area, wider channel or drier climate) or an increase in load (e.g. wetter climate dumping more material into the river or waste disposal).
- ◆ It is an 'explain' question so do not describe.
- ◆ It is not obvious to see how diagrams could help here.

(c) *Suggest two ways in which human activity can cause a river to flood. [6 marks]*

▶▶ See page 6.

- ◆ Asks for 'two ways' so try to make them contrasting ways, e.g. behind a dam versus increased percentage of impermeable surfaces producing more runoff.
- ◆ Doesn't ask for examples but quote some if you know them as it impresses examiners.

(d) *With reference to one or more located examples examine how river channels can be modified to reduce the flood risk. [9 marks]*

▶▶ See page 8.

- ◆ This is the extended question so there is an expectation of a side of A4.
- ◆ One well-chosen example is better than several, i.e. depth is more important than variety.
- ◆ 'Named examples' means located examples – remember to show evidence of place knowledge by naming places and quoting some details (watch your spelling).
- ◆ Clear focus on 'river channels' so don't include river basin approaches such as afforestation of the catchment or land-use planning.
- ◆ 'Modified' – think of the ways (plan, cross section, long section, channel smoothness, channel load, water volume, etc).
- ◆ For nine marks you need to have an example with at least three different types of channel alterations.
- ◆ Don't forget to draw diagrams if it helps the answer.

Chapter 1: Exam café

Essay questions

Remember: you can't do the river environments essay in section B if you have done the river environments question in section A.

With reference to one or more named examples examine why successful management of a river basin requires an understanding of physical processes. [25 marks]

▶▶ See page 10.

◆ The essay tends to come from the later sections of the specification and will normally use wording from the specification as here.

◆ It is an essay so requires an introduction and conclusion. Often conclusions are more important than introductions as they are the last thing the examiner reads and they can be used to pull together the strands of your discussion. They can rescue an 'off-focus' answer.

Student Answer

So I will conclude (1) by saying that if the management of a river basin ignores the physical processes then it will not be successful and could even make it worse (2). In the case of the Mississippi (3) the raising of the levees actually made matters worse as when they broke in 1995 (4) the flooding was even worse.

This is an all too typical conclusion but candidates should:

1 not use the first person nor state the obvious – it creates the wrong impression in the mind of an examiner
2 be specific – make what worse? A sound idea, though
3 always ensure you know how to spell key terms or places
4 avoid repeating something stated elsewhere in the essay.

Clearly this can be improved:

Student Answer

So it can be seen that ignoring the physical processes – river and non-river – can prevent management being successful. In the case of the Mississippi it increased the likelihood of large-scale flooding. It is the unpredictability of these processes and their interaction, such as weathering and mass movement, that must be allowed for in management plans (and their costs) whether these aim to reduce flooding or develop an area for economic activity such as the Thames Gateway project. Nature is a powerful force and should never be ignored but rather it needs understanding.

◆ Again, 'named examples' means located so both examples above had some locational evidence.

◆ Remember that essays need some structure – this is provided by paragraphs having different aspects. In this case it could be different examples of types of physical processes, e.g. weathering or erosion.

◆ Remember that this is about 'successful management' and having an 'understanding' so these should be referred to in the conclusion (as in the second example).

◆ A key element here is to question 'why' so it requires examples to help explain the need to understand the location, scale, frequency and impacts of physical processes found in a river basin.

Chapter 2
Coastal environments

Coastal systems

Coastlines are dynamic systems that at any one time are in a state of change as inputs and outputs change.

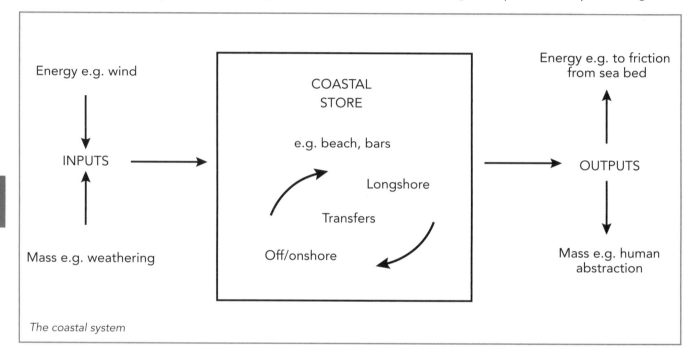

The coastal system

Coastal processes

Student book pages 48–51

Weathering

Weathering is disintegration and decomposition in situ.

Mechanical weathering – no change in state; just disintegrates. For instance:

◆ freeze-thaw – less common as sea keeps coasts mild

◆ salt crystal growth – very common as sea has high salt content

◆ wet/dry – even inter-tidal wet/dry can cause this, especially clays

◆ granular disintegration – some minerals respond more to saltwater

◆ block disintegration

◆ pressure release.

Chemical weathering – change in state just decomposes. For instance:

◆ solution – some rocks dissolve in water, e.g. iron-rich rocks

◆ carbonation – lime-rich rocks dissolve in carbonic acid

◆ oxidation (rusting) – speeds up in moist coastal air

◆ acids – acid rain from pollution (a lot of coastal power stations)

◆ hydrolysis

◆ hydration.

Biological – by plants and animals

Mechanical – roots, coastal birds burrowing in cliffs

Chemical – organic acids from plants, bird droppings, etc.

Mass movement

Mass movement is the movement of material under the force of gravity.

The types of mass movement are usually classified by speed and water content:

◆ Slow – creep
◆ Fast – flows (wet), slides, slumps
◆ Very fast – avalanche, free fall.

┌─ **Key words** ────────────────┐
│   │
│ Sheer strength   Stability slope │
│ Sheer resistance   │
│   │
└────────────────────────────────┘

┌─ **Remember** ─────────────────┐
│   │
│ Mass movement occurs due to the reduction in │
│ sheer strength of the slope and/or an increase │
│ in sheer stress.   │
│   │
└────────────────────────────────┘

Coastal areas (e.g. Barton-on-Sea and Holderness) are prone to mass movement due to the following factors:

◆ Climate – spray and rain increases weight and lubricates
◆ Rock type – soft rocks flow and slide more, e.g. clay
◆ Rock structure – slope of beds is crucial
◆ Relief – steep slopes such as cliffs = more movement
◆ Vegetation – little vegetation as salt kills vegetation
◆ Rate of weathering – high as rocks are exposed in cliffs
◆ Aspect – direction of rain is crucial
◆ Rate of erosion – marine erosion exposes the foot of movement so triggering it. Also, the sea transports any debris away so allowing more to fall
◆ Shock from something to trigger it, e.g. storm waves hitting
◆ Human activity – usually adding weight to slopes such as building housing on cliff tops.

Erosion

Marine erosion can be from wind, ice, river, human activity or the sea itself.

The rate is determined by the energy available and the resistance of surface. Storms and floods increase the rate of erosion. One strong storm can erode more of the coast in a few hours than day-to-day processes in 20 years.

Types of marine erosion:

◆ Abrasion – load is used to wear away cliff, etc
◆ Hydraulic – sheer force and weight of falling water; especially in cracks (air pressure)
◆ Attrition – load collides and grinds away (results in sand)
◆ Solution – removal of chemical ions.

┌─ **Key words** ────────────────┐
│   │
│ Storm surge   Dominant wind │
│ Prevailing wind Longshore drift │
│ Fetch   │
│   │
└────────────────────────────────┘

Factors controlling the rate of marine erosion are:

a) Marine factors:

◆ Depth of water – deeper = more energy
◆ Wave energy – depends on the fetch; bigger fetch = more energy
◆ Tides – small tidal range = more erosion
◆ Direction of prevailing winds and storm frequency
◆ Amount of load carried
◆ Rising sea level.

b) Coastal factors:

◆ Rock type – softer rock erodes more (e.g. clay)
◆ Rock structure – weaknesses like joints are more easily eroded
◆ Rock trend – concordant (Pacific) versus discordant (Atlantic) coastlines. Latter has beds exposed to sea so easily eroded
◆ Angle of dip of the beds – towards the sea = more resistant
◆ Shelter from islands, headlands, etc, absorbs wave energy
◆ Size of beach and coastal vegetation – these absorb wave energy
◆ Relief – higher areas more exposed to other processes.

c) Role of human activity, e.g. level of coastal protection

See page 20.

Case study – The coast at Holderness, Yorkshire.

Transport

Transport could be from wind, ice, rivers, human activity or the sea itself.

The rate is determined by the energy available and the weight of the load. The greater the energy and finer the load, the more that can be carried.

Types of marine transport:
- Floatation – on the surface
- Traction – rolling along the bed
- Saltation – bouncing along the bed
- Solution – dissolved in the water
- Suspension – held in the water.

Key words

Swash zone	Coagulation
Backwash	Evaporation deposits

Coastal material is also transported along the beach (longshore drift) or up the beach (onshore drift). Much coastal material is material pushed onshore by the post-glacial rise in sea level (100m so far and still rising at 1mm a year).

Deposition

Coastal deposition could be from wind, river, human activity or the sea itself.

The rate is determined by the energy loss level and the weight of the load. A shallow gradient, wider beach, calmer climate and meeting a river all slow the waves.

Types of marine deposits:
- Bed load – coarse and dropped first. Cobbles, then pebbles, then sand
- Suspension – silt and sand
- Solution – rarely dropped unless it mixes with salt or in very warm tropical areas where evaporation causes it to precipitate out, usually as lime.

What determines the size, shape and gradient of a beach?
- Material type – pebbles steeper angle of rest than sand
- Type of wave – destructive waves erode steeper beaches
- Tides – often add steps or berms in a beach
- Storms – erode or deposit large amounts
- Human activity – e.g. adding material to beaches to absorb wave energy.

Key words

Berm	Groyne
Stability angle	Replenishment

Remember

Coral is a form of deposition as the creatures precipitate lime out of the sea's solution load to build reefs.

Remember

Marine deposits are easily graded so have long been a source of building materials, chiefly by dredging them from offshore.

Quick check questions

1. Why are coastal areas so prone to mass movement?

2. Why do storms have such an impact on coastal areas?

3. Why is the rate of coastal erosion increasing in the UK?

4. What evidence would help tell you if a beach was the result of longshore or onshore drift?

5. In what ways does the removal of coastal mangrove swamps by humans impact on coastal development?

Factors responsible for coastal processes and landforms

| Student book pages 48–51

Wave factors

These control energy and movement. Wave factors include:

- wave shape – constructive (little backwash so deposits) versus destructive (strong backwash so erodes) or plunging breakers
- wave size – larger waves tend to plunge so erode
- fetch – the greater the fetch the more likely to erode
- roughness – friction slows waves and causes deposition
- depth and gradient – deep water is less likely to deposit
- load – the higher the load the more likely transport and deposition
- tides – large tidal range leads to deposition especially if shallow water
- storm surges – very erosive.

Coastline factors

These dictate the vulnerability of the coastal area. Coastline factors include:

- rock type – soft rocks erode more easily but this adds to load
- structure – hard rocks need weaknesses before they can be eroded
- trend of coast – discordant or concordant
- relief – highland versus lowland
- aspect – the direction the coast faces (compared to prevailing winds)
- human factors – coastal protection, dredging, ports etc.

Time factors

Factors over time relating to the previous sea level, climatic change and tectonic changes:

Features	Sea level fall, e.g. Scotland	Sea level rise, e.g. East Anglia
Reason	Land rising as weight of ice removed	Sea level rising as ice melts
Erosion	Decreased	Increased – rapid cliff erosion
Transport	Longshore more important	Increased onshore transport
Deposition	Little – most offshore	Rapid onshore (bars) and longshore (spits)
Other	Raised beaches Fossil cliff lines Coastal waterfalls Old weathered cliffs Fjord coasts	Drowned river mouths – estuaries and rias (south-west England) Dalmatian coasts – lots of islands

Exam tips

Don't forget that using your fieldwork examples in your answer will impress the examiner.

Quick check questions

1 Why is the fetch of the wave so important?

2 What type of waves produce gentle beaches and why?

3 Which type of coastline is more rapidly eroded – discordant or concordant?

4 What features are associated with offshore bars?

5 When a bar comes onshore, what does it form?

Coastal features

You should be able to **describe** coastal features (i.e. their shape, size, location and composition) and **explain** how they were formed. The most effective way is with well-annotated diagrams.

Most questions ask you to describe and explain two features of either erosion or deposition:

Erosion features

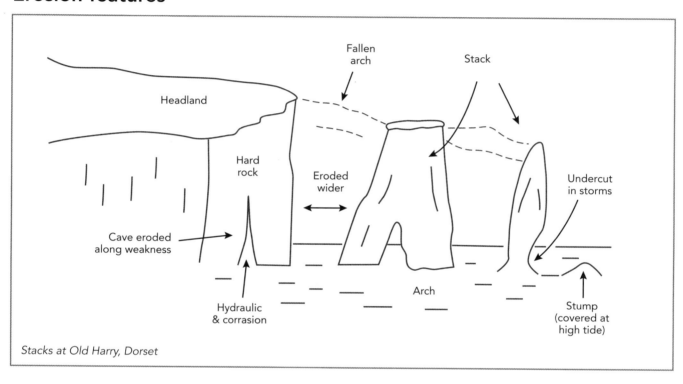

Stacks at Old Harry, Dorset

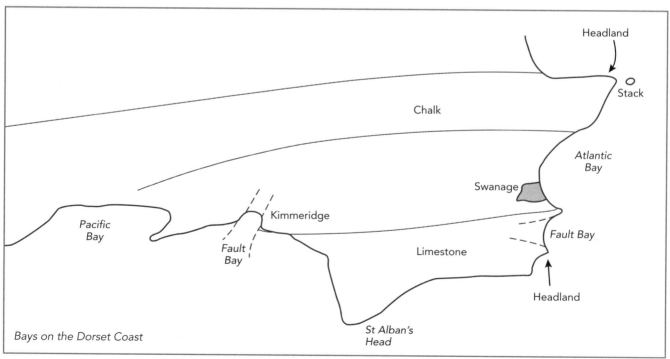

Bays on the Dorset Coast

Chapter 2: Coastal environments

18

Depositititon features

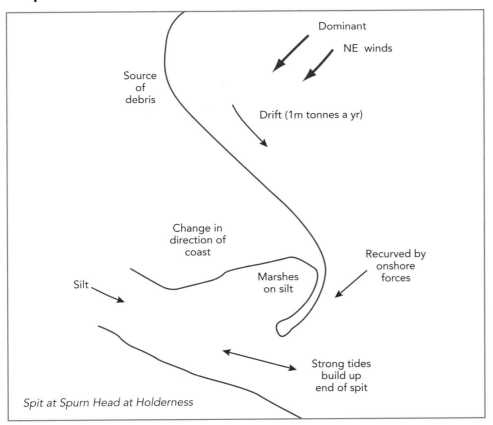

Dominant

NE winds

Source of debris

Drift (1m tonnes a yr)

Change in direction of coast

Silt

Marshes on silt

Recurved by onshore forces

Strong tides build up end of spit

Spit at Spurn Head at Holderness

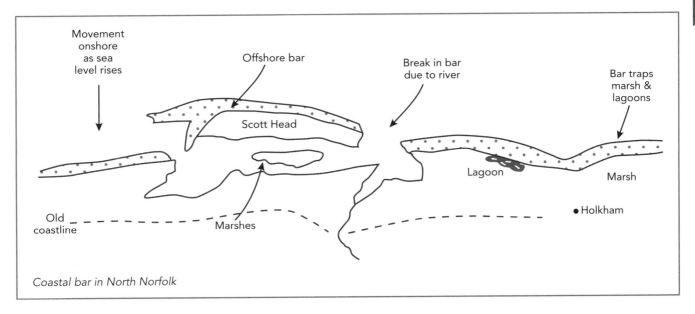

Movement onshore as sea level rises

Offshore bar

Break in bar due to river

Bar traps marsh & lagoons

Scott Head

Lagoon

Marsh

Old coastline

Marshes

• Holkham

Coastal bar in North Norfolk

How coasts can be protected

Student book pages 58–71

Remember

Relate these factors to the inputs, outputs, flows and stores of the coastal systems diagram on page 14.

Why some coasts need protecting

Physical reasons:

◆ Climate – global warming leading to rising sea level and more storms
◆ Relief – low-lying areas are at risk
◆ Aspect – open to large wave fetch
◆ Depth of water – deep water inshore allows more erosive waves to break
◆ Drainage – deltas and estuaries combine river and marine flooding threats

- Vegetation – loss of protective mangrove swamps, e.g. Sri Lanka
- Ecosystem – rare and fragile, e.g. salt marshes in UK, reefs in Australia
- Geology – weak rocks prone to erosion and mass movement, e.g. Barton-on-Sea.

Human reasons:

- Settlement – there are a lot of expensive coastal properties at risk
- Source of raw materials, e.g. sand and gravel extraction off Hall sands
- Industrial and power station sites need protecting, e.g. nuclear plants in UK
- Transport needs protecting, e.g. coastal road on Spurn Head, railway at Teignmouth, Devon
- Ports need protecting from silting, e.g. Kings Lynn, Norfolk
- Jobs – create jobs using schemes
- Fishing – protect fishing grounds and shellfish, e.g. oyster areas
- Military ranges threaten the area, e.g. Pembrokeshire, Wales
- Tourism and recreation – protect the beach from erosion, e.g. Southwold, Suffolk
- Cultural and historic sites, e.g. loss of Dunwich in Suffolk.

Case study: Holderness

> Student book page 56

At Holderness, a coastline of 61km stretches south from the chalk cliffs of Flamborough Head. It is being eroded the most rapidly in Europe at 2m a year. 4km has been lost since Roman times.

Factors affecting erosion	Holderness
Natural:	
Climate	Open to strong north-east winds which have a large fetch so strong destructive waves
Relief	Low cliffs 3–35m in height
Aspect	Open to strongest winter winds. No shelter
Depth of water	Deep water – 10m at only 600m from the beach
Drainage	Poorly drained so cliffs easily mass move (slips and flows)
Vegetation	Salt winds reduce tree numbers that would bind the cliff with their roots
Geology	Very soft glacial deposits (till)
Other	Much of the material is taken offshore – only 3% feeds Spurn Head. Flamborough Head stops drift from the north
Human:	
Sea defences	These have reduced coastal drift so preventing the build-up of protective beach material at cliff foot
Cost/benefit	It would be very expensive to protect 61km especially as population is patchy along the coast

Methods of protection

Hard engineering (e.g. Ventnor, Isle of Wight)

> Student book pages 68–69

- Sea walls – some curved to reflect wave energy back on itself
- Groynes – trap sand which acts as a cushion to wave energy
- Rock armour (rip-rap – large rocks)
- Gabions (steel mesh cages with small rocks)
- Revetments (wood or concrete – absorb energy but let water through)
- Offshore bars (boulders, tyres etc designed to break waves)
- Tetrapods (concrete 'jacks' – act like rip-rap).

Exam tips

Shoreline management plans assess whether costs and benefits suggest 'hold the line' or 'managed retreat' is the best strategy.

Key words

Sediment cell	Gabion
Coastal squeeze	Revetment
Groyne	

However, hard engineering is:

◆ expensive – up to £8 million per km

◆ unsightly and may restrict access

◆ not environmentally friendly

◆ majorly disruptive due to construction

◆ often the cause of unforeseen effects further along the coast

◆ in need of ongoing expensive maintenance.

Soft engineering (e.g. Pevensey Bay)

> Student book pages 66–67

◆ Beach replenishment – adding sand from offshore dredging

◆ Beach re-cycling (moving beach material about, e.g. from downdrift)

◆ Beach or cliff re-profiling – material bulldozed back up the beach

◆ Groyne replacement – many removed

◆ Fencing – limits access and traps blowing sand

◆ Planting vegetation – binds cliffs or sand dunes.

Soft engineering is cheaper and more natural than hard engineering. It may add value by improving the beach for tourists.

Managed retreat or realignment (e.g. Abbotts Hall Farm, Essex)

> Student book pages 70–71

Land is allowed to flood and it forms salt marshes that absorb wave energy. Managed retreat is cheap and natural but requires an area with little or no population.

Coastal areas are often protected by a combination of these approaches:

◆ Cliff foot protection

◆ Cliff face protection

◆ Cliff top protection.

(See Barton-on-Sea example below.)

Coastal areas as a valuable economic and environmental resource

> Student book pages 72–73

Why are coastal areas so attractive?

◆ Scenery – tourism

◆ Mild climate – retirement

◆ Access to water – recreation

◆ Economic activities, e.g. fishing

◆ Cheap coastal transport

◆ Raw materials – sand etc

◆ Flat land (cliffed areas are not so attractive).

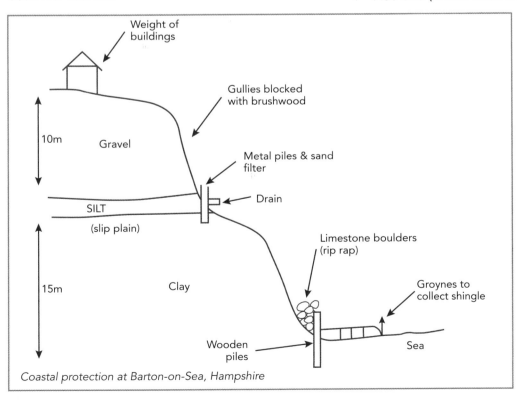

Coastal protection at Barton-on-Sea, Hampshire

Types of activity attracted to coastal areas:

◆ Power – tide mills, tidal power station (proposed for the Severn estuary)
◆ Industry – fishing, flat land ideal for heavy industry, etc
◆ Water supply cooling (but salt is a problem)
◆ Settlement – flat land, views, retired and holiday homes
◆ Services – tourism, recreation, waste disposal
◆ Minerals and sediments – gravel/sand, oil/gas
◆ Agriculture – mild climate so early vegetables, etc, grazing on saltmarshes, fish farms
◆ Transport – ports, bulk cargoes
◆ Conservation – saltmarshes, marshlands, nature reserves.

Exam tips

Try to ensure your two case studies are contrasting in some respect, e.g. highland versus lowland or MEDC versus LEDC.

Quick check questions

1 What in your opinion is the main reason why the Holderness coast is being so rapidly eroded?

2 Why is the Holderness coastline not better protected from erosion by the sea?

3 Why might people object to rip-raps being used to protect a beach?

4 Many dune areas are stabilised with vegetation. What conflicts could this cause?

5 What do you think is the main objection to managed retreat?

Case study: two coastal areas

Student book pages 72–73

	Southampton Water and the Solent (MEDC)	Bahia, north-east Brazil (LEDC/NIC)
Power	Site of Fawley oil-fired power station and Marchwood	Power station at Camacari
Industry	Bulky industries such as oil refining Exxon, Petro-chemicals at Fawley, fertiliser plant. New hi-tech industry attracted as suits specialist workforce. Some fishing	Bulky industries such as oil refining , Petro-chemicals at Camacari. Assembly industries (import components), cars at Camacari. Still some fishing
Water supply	Used in power stations and refinery for cooling	Used in power stations and refinery for cooling
Settlement	Major city/port at Southampton. Major retirement area, e.g. Lymington	High population in coastal strip. Major city of Salvador
Services	Recreation and leisure, e.g. Calshot activities centre, Cowes and Hamble Marinas, holiday villages, e.g. Thorness	Rapid growth as tourist area – vast beaches at Port Segura and Seripe. £200 million investment. Praia do Forte is Brazil's first eco-resort.
Minerals	Sand and gravel	Sand, gravel. Oil and gas offshore
Agriculture	Market gardening for Southampton market	Main area for sugar, cocoa and tobacco
Transport	Container deep water port Roll on/roll off facility Bulk terminal Three cruise terminals	Salvador has a container port, bulk terminal and is Brazil's largest fruit exporter
Conservation	Dibden bay mudflats include several SSSIs and the Keyhaven nature reserve of saltmarshes	Increasing – 2006 Sauipe Park conservation area and eco-resort based on lagoons and coral reefs
Waste disposal	Waste warm water from refinery and power stations dumped in Southampton water	Most sewage and industrial waste dumped in sea

Conflicts between land uses

Student book pages 72–73

Conflicts may be because:

◆ one activity impacts on another, e.g. wildlife disturbed by motorboats

◆ activities compete to use the same water, e.g. fishing versus cooling water

◆ an activity changes the nature of the water for another user, e.g. industrial water pollution of water for tourism.

Other conflicts arise as water is a fluid so moves from one area to another with its contents (e.g. fish).

Some conflicts occur between users of the mobile water and fixed seabed, e.g. oil exploitation. They can be:

◆ between different land uses/activities; e.g. Southampton water – oil refinery and conservation area (saltmarshes behind Calshot Spit)

◆ within the same land use/activity, e.g. Bahia – recreation sees conflicts between wind surfers, swimmers, power boats, sailing, jet skis and game fishing.

 See page 6.

Case study: Thames Estuary (Chapter 1 River Environments).

Management challenges associated with coastal development

Student book pages 74–83

Management challenges include how to balance the following factors against each other:

◆ Environmental needs (e.g. wildlife, reefs, vegetation)

◆ Economic factors (e.g. tourism, settlement, transport)

◆ Social factors (e.g. people's sense of safety, security of property, pleasant scenery, historic/cultural aspects).

Key words

Sustainability

Conservation

SMPs

Issues of management

Issues of managing coastal development include:

◆ What is the exact nature of the coastal and marine resources and their status (quality versus quantity)? We lack data on most coastal areas.

◆ Sheer cost: short versus long term, e.g. the West Bay Dorset protection cost £20 million. Who should pay? Local versus national issue – rate payer (or visitor) versus tax payer.

◆ Who pays versus who gains ? Should tax payers subsidise developments that benefit a small group, e.g. retired home owners? The problems at Fairlight (East Sussex) well exemplify this. How effective is the scheme and for whom?

◆ Political will. For instance, one authority may be affected by the management of another updrift, e.g. Bournemouth (Dorset) altered the beach at Barton (Hampshire) by building a large groyne.

◆ Ownership – who is responsible for the coast? Most is privately owned but some is owned by the army or charities (e.g. National Trust). How far does the coast extend inland?

◆ Technology – does the region possess the knowledge and expertise to manage the area? Is enough known about that particular coast and sediment cell(s)?

◆ Size or scale – definition of the area that makes up the stretch of coastline. It is easier to manage smaller coasts, e.g. Mediterranean coastline is 46,000km long.

◆ How long will it take? Quick fix versus long term; e.g. many sea walls will not cope with the forecast rise in the sea level.

◆ Wider impacts. What implications are there for areas beyond the coast, e.g. rivers or estuarine areas, or areas further inland? Why should governments concentrate on the thin coastal strip at the expense of the rest of the area or country?

Exam tips

When asked about coastal management schemes try to use contrasting examples in the scale, ownership or type of management agency.

Types of management

Single agency: e.g. National Trust, Army, individual landowner

The National Trust started Enterprise Neptune to protect 1000 miles of coastline in England, Wales and Northern Ireland (about a third of the total coastline) which was of natural beauty. By 2007 over 700 miles were directly owned by the Trust and so protected from development (e.g. Giant's Causeway, Northern Ireland). The area is managed by the Trust to maintain its beauty and yet allow visitor access (e.g. Studland Beach in Dorset).

National or Regional Park: e.g. Pembrokeshire Coast

The Pembrokeshire National Park was set up in 1952. It is a 240km stretch of coast 629km² in area. It includes many sites of national or international conservation significance including seven Special Areas of Conservation, three Special Protection Areas, a Marine Nature Reserve, six National Nature Reserves and 75 Sites of Special Scientific Interest. The National Park doesn't own the land but is the planning and highway authority. It is charged with managing a living environment so must balance environmental and economic forces.

Integrated regional planning: e.g. Shoreline Management Planning by DEFRA

> **Student book pages 63–65**

DEFRA introduced the original guidance in 1995 and shoreline management plans (SMPs) now cover the entire shoreline of England and Wales. A SMP

Quick check questions

1. Why are 'sediment cells' important when undertaking coastal management schemes?
2. Do you think the private ownership of coastal areas is an effective way of protecting the coastline from erosion? Justify your answer.
3. What is the main way National Parks can protect a coastal area from development?
4. What do the initials DEFRA mean?
5. Why might the notion of a cost–benefit analysis in coastal management be challenged by local people?

is a large-scale assessment of the risks associated with coastal processes and helps to reduce these risks to people and the developed, historic and natural environment. These were based on distinctive sediment cells to minimise impacts of schemes on other areas. They were designed to manage coastal flood risks and erosion and schemes had to be related to cost–benefit.

Integrated national or international planning: e.g. Integrated Coastal Zone Management by the EU in the Mediterranean

> **Student book pages 82–83**

In 1975 the Mediterranean Action Plan was set up as part of the United Nation's Environmental Programme. In 2006 the EU launched an initiative to clean up the Mediterranean by 2020 – the Blue Plan.

Case study: the Mediterranean

The environmental pressures on the coast	The strategy – the Blue Plan
Increasing population leading to increased urbanisation	Development of green areas to separate urban development
Development of coastal resorts, airports, etc	Inland tourism to be encouraged and increased sustainability in coastal resorts. All new development to include environmental protection in its planning
Damage to fragile wetlands, e.g. the Camargue	10% of all coastal and marine habitats to be protected
Removal of sand and gravel has damaged seabed habitats	Stricter control on dredging and extraction
Increase in size and number of oil tankers	Stricter rules and fines to reduce tanker pollution
Agri-chemicals are polluting coastal areas – algae blooms	Tighter controls on the use of agri-chemicals
Untreated waste dumping	All waste water to be fully treated before discharge
Industrial effluent	All waste water to be fully treated before discharge

Exam**Café**

Sample questions

1

(a) *Outline the ways in which the sea carries its load.* *[4 marks]*

▶▶ See page 15.
- ◆ 'Outline' means no need to describe in detail.
- ◆ 'Outline' does not require you to explain.
- ◆ Four marks usually means there are at least four methods (there are) or to do two in detail.
- ◆ An annotated diagram would help to show where these 'ways' operate, e.g. traction along the seabed.

(b) *Explain the conditions that lead to coastal deposition.* *[6 marks]*

▶▶ See page 16.
- ◆ Compare the wording of the river equivalent – not the same but the same thrust so they are deemed comparable.
- ◆ Six marks normally needs at least two conditions. In reality there is only one here – a loss of carrying capacity. This could be due to a loss of energy (meets the coast, loss of water depth, meets a river, becomes sheltered from the wind, etc) or an increase in load (wetter climate dumping more material into the sea, increased coastal erosion, waste disposal, etc).
- ◆ It is an explanation question so do not describe.
- ◆ It is not obvious to see how diagrams could help here but examples would impress the examiner.

(c) *Suggest two ways in which environmental factors may increase the risk of coastal flooding.* *[6 marks]*

▶▶ See page 19.
- ◆ Again, not identical to, but in very much the same spirit as the river environments question.
- ◆ Environmental normally means physical but could include human.
- ◆ 'Two ways' so try to make them contrasting ways, e.g. physical such as rising sea level versus removal of offshore sand/gravel for the construction industry.
- ◆ Doesn't ask for examples but quote some if you know them as it impresses examiners.

(d) *With reference to one or more located examples, examine how coasts can be managed to reduce coastal erosion.* *[9 marks]*

▶▶ See page 20.
- ◆ This the extended question so there is an expectation of a side of A4.
- ◆ One example well chosen is better than several, i.e. depth is more important than variety. Here a comparison would be better – soft versus hard engineering, for example.
- ◆ 'Named examples' means located examples – remember to show evidence of place knowledge by naming places and quoting some details (watch your spelling).
- ◆ Clear focus on coasts so don't go far inland.
- ◆ 'Managed' – think of the ways (soft, hard, managed retreat).
- ◆ For nine marks you need to refer to at least three different types of management, i.e. gabions and use of groynes would be treated as two.
- ◆ Don't forget to draw diagrams if it helps the answer. Barton would be ideal.

Essay questions

Remember: you can't do the coastal environments essay in section B if you have done the coastal environments question in section A.

With reference to one or more named examples, examine why coastal management schemes may need to resolve conflicts in such areas. [25 marks]

▶▶ See page 24.

◆ The essay tends (but not always) to come from the later sections of the specification and will normally use wording from the specification. Here it takes the spirit of the last section rather than the exact wording.

◆ It is an essay so requires an introduction and conclusion. Often conclusions are more important than introductions as they are the last thing the examiner reads and they can be used to pull together the strands of your discussion. They can rescue an 'off-focus' answer.

Student Answer

So I will conclude (1) by saying that if a coastal management scheme ignores the environment conflicts and other human activities in the area it will not be successful and could even make it worse (2). In the case of the groyne at Bornemouth (3) the trapping of the sand actually made matters worse for downdrift areas such as Barton(4) where the level of erosion was increased.

This is an all too typical conclusion but candidates should:

(1) not use the first person nor state the obvious – it creates the wrong impression in the mind of an examiner
(2) be specific – make what worse? A sound idea, though
(3) always ensure you know how to spell key terms or places
(4) avoid repeating something stated elsewhere in the essay.

Clearly this can be improved:

Student Answer

Coastal management schemes are rarely multi-purpose, being largely focused on coastal protection, but they nearly always impact on a vast range of coastal users who may not share the same goals and may conflict with various environmental factors. All too often a scheme in one area has unforeseen impacts on areas updrift and downdrift of the scheme leading to increased conflicts. Also, conflicts may occur over time as short-term actions have long-term impacts as in the case of Hall Sands. It always pays to research the coastal processes and potential conflicts before embarking on any such scheme rather than trying to resolve them afterwards.

◆ Again, 'named examples' means located so both examples above had some locational evidence.

◆ Remember that essays need some structure – this is provided by paragraphs having different aspects. In this case it could be different examples of types of conflicts caused – with neighbouring areas, with tourists, residents, fishermen, etc.

◆ Remember that this is about 'may need to resolve' so this should be referred to in the conclusion (as in the second example).

Chapter 3
Cold environments

Defining cold climates

Student book pages 90–91

Cold climates are those with a distinct season below freezing – with snow in winter.

They can be defined by latitude (resulting from high latitude – more radiation lost than gained due to Earth's curvature):

- Polar (arctic and subarctic) climates, e.g. Antarctica in winter –70°C and in summer –20°C. Dry 100mm
- Periglacial (tundra), e.g. Siberia in winter –50°C and in summer 16°C. Dry 160mm
- Coniferous forest (taiga/boreal), e.g. northern Sweden in winter –25°C and in summer 16°C. Dry 320mm.

Cold climates can also be defined by altitude (temperature loses 1°C per 100m rise as the air is thinner away from the Earth's re-radiated heat and it's windier):

- Mountain (alpine), e.g. Colorado Springs, USA in winter –10°C and in summer 18°C. Dry 567mm.

Key words

Insolation	Tundra
Katabatic wind	Diurnal
Periglacial	

Many areas were cold climates in the relatively recent past so show evidence of cold climate landforms, e.g. much of Europe following the last ice age.

Remember

Areas such as North Wales, the Grampians and the Lake District once had these climates so expect OS map questions.

Climatic features include:

- Low precipitation as cold air can't hold much moisture
- Heavy winter snowfall (remember 1mm of rain = 12mm of snow)
- Cold winters with intense frosts but mild summers
- Little cloud (relatively dry air) so long sunshine hours
- Strong winds – often local via valleys or off glaciers (katabatic winds).

Processes at work in cold environments

Student book pages 92–110

Weathering

Weathering in cold environments can be mechanical, chemical or biological:

Mechanical – no change in state; just disintegrates usually as a result of sudden temperature changes. For instance:

- freeze-thaw – water gets into cracks and expands 9 per cent when it freezes
- wet/dry – glacial clays crack up in cold dry winters
- pressure release – as glaciers melt.

Chemical – change in state just decomposes (slow as cold); usually following snow melt due to dampness. For instance:

- solution/carbonation – limestone dissolves more rapidly in cold temperatures
- acid action – especially if snow is polluted
- hydrolysis – water reacts with minerals to produce clays.

Biological – by plants and animals (usually in a search for water, nutrients or shelter).

Glaciers (past and present)

Why is ice so effective in cold environments?

◆ Rock is bare with little soil or vegetation due to cold temperature

◆ Other processes are slowed, e.g. rivers freeze

◆ Ice is a semi-solid so is a powerful erosive tool

◆ Sheer volume and size

◆ Ice fills valleys eroding sides and base (unlike a river which cuts downwards).

Types of erosion:

◆ Plucking – ice freezes to rock and pulls it off as it moves

◆ Abrasion – debris in ice is used like sandpaper

◆ Bulldozing – pushing already weathered rock debris.

What controls the rate of erosion by the glacier?

◆ Speed of ice movement – the faster the movement, the greater the erosion

◆ Temperature of the lower ice – if below freezing it sticks so little erosion

◆ Thickness of ice – thicker ice erodes more due to weight

◆ Debris – large angular debris erodes more

◆ Basal water – if there is water at the base of the ice, it slides so little erosion

◆ Nature of the bedrock – soft bedrock erodes quicker

◆ Pre-existing relief – narrow valleys eroded more as the ice is under more pressure.

Evidence of erosion by glaciers includes: scratches on rocks (striations), polished rocks, erratics (rocks of a different geology to that in the area) and valley and landform shapes.

Key words

Congelifraction	Ablation
Nivation	Striations

Glaciers also deposit once they are slowed, such as following friction along the valley side or melt – resulting from moving to warmer areas, climate change or meeting warm water bodies, e.g. the sea.

The types of glacial deposit depend on where it is carried in the glacier:

◆ On top: ablation till – coarse, angular

◆ Underneath: lodgement till – fine, crushed, less angular.

Remember

All these processes of erosion can also transport debris but then will deposit it once energy is lost.

Water erosion and deposition

Why is water a major factor in cold environments?

◆ Summer melt can be sudden

◆ Lots of debris for water to carry and use

◆ High capacity as little initial load

◆ Often ponded glacial lakes released on glacial melt – high energy

◆ Ground is frozen (permafrost) so is impervious.

Wind erosion and deposition

Why is wind so effective in cold environments?

◆ Extreme pressure differences – glaciers are cold so air above sinks to form intense high pressure areas

◆ Little vegetation to slow wind

◆ Lots of fine debris (sand) from mechanical weathering.

Periglacial

This results from permafrost (permanently frozen ground usually on the edge of the glacier or before and after a glacial period). Processes at work include:

◆ Usually only the top layer of ground (active layer) thaws in summer

◆ Expansion features – water freezes and expands, e.g. Pingo

◆ Contraction features – if temperatures get very low, the ice contracts, e.g. ice wedges

◆ Mass movement – sludging of thawed soil, e.g. solifluction

◆ Seasonal river flows cause braids

◆ Wind action – erosion (sculptured rocks) deposition (dunes, loess).

Key words

Permafrost	Solifluction
Active layer	Congeliturbation

1 Why do cold areas get heavy snow falls when precipitation totals are low?

2 Is all chemical weathering slowed by cold temperatures? Explain your answer.

3 What evidence for abrasion by glaciers would you look for?

4 Why are temperate glaciers relatively fast movers but cause little erosion of the bedrock?

5 How would you distinguish glacial deposits from fluvio-glacial deposits?

Features of cold areas

You should be able to **describe** features of cold areas, i.e. their shape, size, location, composition, and **explain** how they were formed. The most effective way is with well-annotated diagrams.

Features result from:

◆ **W**eathering – frost action, snow action (nivation), wet/dry, pressure release, hot/cold, vegetation, solution, acid action

◆ **E**rosion – glacial (bulldozing, plucking, abrasion), meltwater, wind action

◆ **T**ransport – mass movement (solifluction, frost heave, avalanche, creep, flows, slides), meltwater, ice, wind

◆ **D**eposition – glacial (lodgement, ablation, englacial), meltwater, wind.

Student book pages 96–110

Most questions ask you to describe and explain two features from:

Glacial erosion:

◆ Cirques

◆ U-shaped valleys

Glacial deposition:

◆ Moraines

◆ Outwash plains.

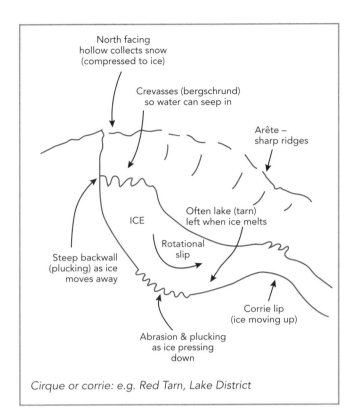

Cirque or corrie: e.g. Red Tarn, Lake District

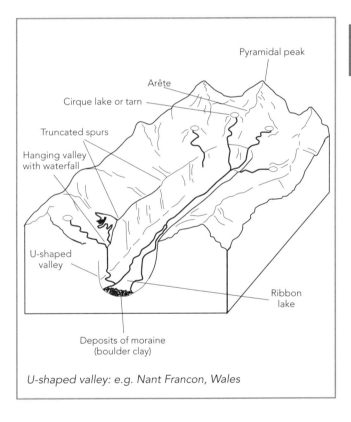

U-shaped valley: e.g. Nant Francon, Wales

29

Chapter 3: Cold environments

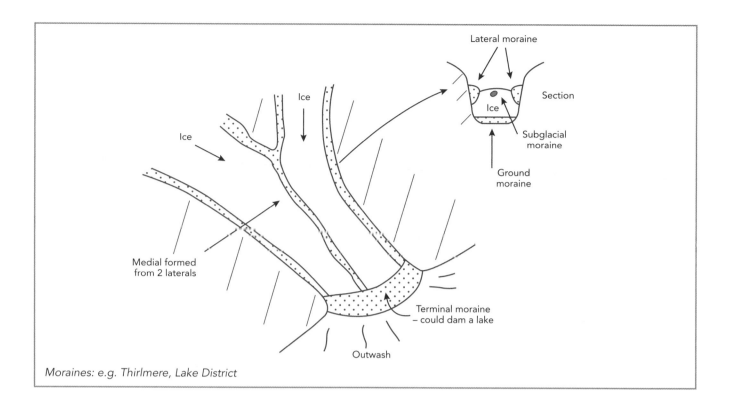

Moraines: e.g. Thirlmere, Lake District

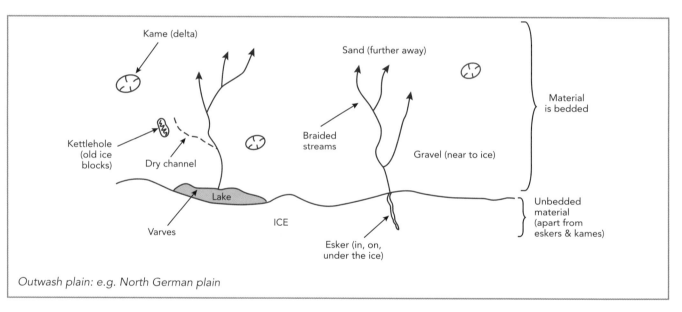

Outwash plain: e.g. North German plain

Remember

A well-labelled diagram saves a lot of words in an exam. Labelling (annotation) is more important than the artistic nature of the diagram.

Exam tips

You are not required to know periglacial landforms but many of the processes are challenges to development in cold areas.

Quick check questions

1 What features are usually found in U-shaped valleys?

2 Why are few cirques (corries) found on south-facing slopes?

3 What is a tarn?

4 How could you distinguish a push terminal moraine?

5 Why is it more difficult to identify glacial depositional features in lowland areas than highland areas?

Impact of climate on the ecosystem

Student book pages 112–15

Plants and animals have to adapt to:

- very cold seasons with hard frosts
- strong winds and wind chill
- prolonged drought; especially in winter when water frozen
- heavy snowfalls – weight, but does insulate ground/vegetation beneath
- competition for food, water and shelter
- a large number and variety of consumers.

Plants adapt by:

- size – low lying so close to warmer ground and snow insulates
- roots – large underground system to store food
- stems – thin but tough to withstand grazing and wind. Succulents store water
- leaves – small and waxy to avoid frost damage and water loss
- life cycle – very quick or longer living than annuals. Make use of long summer daylight
- reproduction – usually by bulbs or layering as safer than flowers, e.g. lichen and heather.

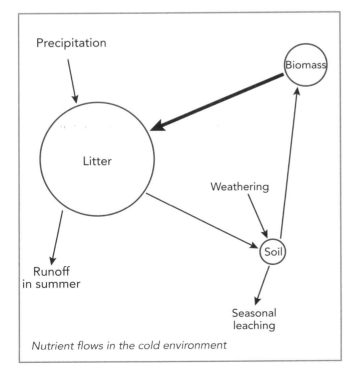

Nutrient flows in the cold environment

Animals adapt by:

- size – small to reduce heat and water loss
- habit – many migrate (e.g. caribou), hibernate (e.g. bears), live underground to avoid cold or live in the warmer sea (e.g. seals)
- bodies – small and fur/hair to reduce heat and water loss
- blood systems – often contain a type of antifreeze
- feet – insulated with fur pads as ground cold
- food – can store food as body fat
- life cycle – compressed breeding cycle with large number of offspring, e.g. lemming
- other ways – some change colour to white in winter, e.g. arctic hare, marmot, arctic fox.

Key words

Perennials
Net primary productivity
Gley soil

Why so fragile?

Is the environment fragile or does it suffer oscillations?

Remember

Remember food chains/webs – these tend to be short. Many species have very distinct ways of surviving (niche species).

Causes of fragility:

- Extreme climate with 'sudden' events, e.g. a very cold or very warm snap, blizzards
- Dry climates
- Delicate nature of permafrost (global warming) – waterlogged soils
- Low energy environment (low inputs – cold)
- Low nutrient stores as weathering slow due to cold and vulnerable flows
- Limited range of species – limited gene pool and food chains
- Largely undisturbed until 20th century.

Remember

The nutrient stores and flows will vary a little with the exact nature of the cold environment.

Case study: The Alps, Switzerland

Student book page 114

	Examples of threats to ecosystem
Natural threats	
Climatic	Global warming melting permafrost
Landslides and floods	Mass movements and floods destroy habitats
Fire	Increasing in dry summers
Human threats	
Urbanisation	Construction of ski resorts, transmitters, etc
Transport	Building of roads to reach the resorts and pollution
Industry	Building of dams has changed river regimes
Recreation	Skiing, snow boarding, etc, damages slopes and vegetation
Mining	Quarrying and mining destroy the environment
Farming	Overgrazing by sheep and goats
Other	Forest clearance has increased avalanches and runoff

Quick check questions

1 Why are small plants better suited than big plants to cold environments?

2 How do trees survive in cold environments?

3 Which is the smallest nutrient store in cold ecosystems and why?

4 How do large animals like grizzly bears survive in cold environments?

5 Why are warm or mild winters so damaging to cold environment ecosystems?

Opportunities and challenges in developing cold environments

Student book pages 118–22

Opportunities both attract development to cold environments and are in turn the result of development, e.g. oil in Alaska was an opportunity to be developed, and its development created numerous further opportunities such as transport, building etc. Likewise, challenges hinder, slow or alter the nature of the development. Equally, however, development can create challenges such as the urgent need to protect the rapidly disappearing permafrost.

Opportunities include:

◆ power production – wind, hydro

◆ industry – tourism, furs

◆ settlement – military and research bases, resorts

◆ mining – oil, gas, ores, quarrying

◆ agriculture – reindeer, grazing cattle and sheep

◆ forestry – on fringes

◆ military bases and exercises.

Case studies: Northern Sweden and Siberia

Student book pages 120–21

1. Resources

	Northern Sweden – the Sami	Siberia – oil
Facts	Between 70,000 and 100,000 people in northern Norway, Sweden and Finland. Since 1991 had own parliament. Two groups – reindeer herders and sea Sami (fishing)	Over 600 fields with reserves of 144 billion barrels and 1200 trillion cubic feet of gas. 70% of Russia's output. Massive expansion since 1990s with pipelines to Europe and China
Environmental impact	◆ Minimal – migrated with seasons and kept herds in line with carrying capacity ◆ Increasingly restricted by mining, forest clearance and hydro schemes	◆ Massive pollution of soil, lakes and groundwater from spills; e.g. 1994 – over 50 million gallons and leaking pipelines ◆ Habitats destroyed by road building, pipe line laying and hunting for food. ◆ Damage to permafrost by pumping – subsidence
Economic impact	◆ Low income so many migrate to cities for work ◆ Few roads or towns as tribes were nomadic ◆ Few services as largely self-sufficient ◆ Subsistence with reindeer supplying most of their needs	◆ Urbanisation – e.g. Khanty-Mansiysk, Surgut ◆ $4.5 billion in tax revenue ◆ Highly-paid, skilled jobs ◆ New roads and airports ◆ New services, e.g. hospitals ◆ New cash farming under heated glass
Social impact	◆ Increasingly absorbed into westernised way of life (only 10% now live off herds) ◆ Becoming a tourist attraction ◆ Tribal organisation being weakened	◆ Local Khanty and Selkup people lost their reindeer herds and can't migrate due to pipelines = increased depression, Aids, suicide and alcoholism ◆ Influx of foreign workers
Political impact	◆ Lost land rights last century so forced out of private forests where reindeer sheltered but now legally protected	◆ Local village headmen replaced by state or oil company control ◆ Corruption and violence ◆ Government see energy as a political power tool
Cultural impact	◆ Being protected and Sami parliament fosters language and culture	◆ Khanty lost links to their land ◆ Destruction of sacred places ◆ Influx of new more westernised workers and cultures

2. Recreation and tourism

	Antarctica	Skiing in Switzerland
Facts	80,000 tourists a year expected by 2010	Alps receive 100 million tourists a year – 60% for winter sports
Environmental impact	Concentrated round certain bases so concentrates pollution, disturbance to habitats, etc Tourist ships disturb sea life especially whales (noise, wash and waste)	Skiers damage trees, kill young shoots and erode surfaces Car exhaust fumes kill trees Access roads, parking lifts, etc, destroy habitats Increased risk of avalanche Litter Bulldozing of slopes Increased water use and sewage disposal
Economic impact	Very little as all money spent outside area Size of bases is controlled Tourist ships are largely self-sufficient	Creation of jobs (80% of jobs rely on tourism) Building of resorts Destruction of traditional farming Higher incomes but also higher prices Improved infrastructure
Social impact	Minimal as the local population is very small and these people do not live there permanently	Local people priced out of their own homes Influx of foreign young seasonal workers
Political impact	Some conflicts due to overlapping claims of control, e.g. UK and Argentina	Who pays for the infrastructure and damaged environment?
Cultural impact	No existing culture	Any traditional culture survives as a tourist attraction

Key words

Infrastructure   Thermokarst

Nomadism

Remember

What will happen when the oil and gas run out? Is the development sustainable without high investments of money and technology?

Challenges

Physical challenges:

- Climate – harsh and extreme, cold and dry
- Climate change – melting the permafrost
- Relief – steep or flat due to glacial action and periglacial deposits
- Vegetation – thin and tough, difficult to use or clear
- Drainage – role of permafrost; poor drainage/ waterlogging
- Ecosystem – hostile, limited or low productivity
- Soils – leached by seasonal thaw, permafrost
- Permafrost is a vast store of carbon dioxide.

Human challenges:

- Low population – few want to live there
- High-cost environment to offset climate
- Building difficult due to permafrost
- Remote and land transport difficult, especially in winter
- Pollution threats, e.g. oil
- Over-hunting
- Existing indigenous populations with their own culture
- Need for conservation of endangered habitats.

How can cold areas be managed sustainably?

Student book pages 123–25

The management challenge

Key words

Sustainable	Conservation
Cost-benefit	Preservation

The management challenge involves how to balance the environmental needs (e.g. wildlife, hydrology, vegetation) against economic factors (e.g. farming, employment, transport) and social factors (e.g. pleasant scenery, historic/cultural aspects).

Issues:

◆ What is the exact nature of the environmental and water resources and their status? Little research on permafrost.

◆ Sheer cost – short versus long term. Who should pay – locals or tourists? Local versus national issue – rate payer (or water board) versus tax payer.

◆ Who pays versus who gains? Should tax payers subsidise developments that benefit a small group, e.g. skiers? How effective is the scheme and for whom?

◆ Political will, e.g. the Alps covers parts of at least eight countries. Ownership – who is responsible for rivers flowing through such areas? E.g. the Rhine starts in the Swiss Alps, a non-EU country, but flows through France, Germany and the Netherlands.

◆ Technology – has the area the knowledge and expertise to develop the challenging environment? Is enough known about that particular environment and its climate?

◆ Size or scale – definition of the area that makes up the area to be managed.

◆ How long will it take? Quick fix versus long term.

◆ Wider impacts. What implications are there for areas beyond the area, e.g. changes in the Alps have implications for the Netherlands?

Special problems of permafrost areas include:

◆ Buildings' heat may thaw permafrost beneath so buildings subside

◆ Permafrost is rock solid in winter but very soft and waterlogged in summer

◆ Pipelines have to be above ground or they melt the permafrost

◆ Roads have thick layers of gravel to insulate them from permafrost but frequently they buckle and sink

◆ Waterlogged summer soils encourage vast swarms of insects, e.g. midges

◆ Waste disposal is difficult – can melt permafrost

◆ Ground may swell or shrink producing 'drunken' forests or telephone poles.

Key words

Active layer	Insulation
Avalanche	Thermokarst

Remember

Remember that traditional indigenous populations have successfully lived in these areas for centuries by adapting to the conditions.

There are two approaches to management:
1. Manage to fit (adapt to the conditions or adapt the conditions)
2. Conserve to prevent (protect at all costs).

Adapting to the conditions is:

◆ cheap – often low-level technology will be effective, e.g. dog sledge

◆ easily understood and needs little skill/education

◆ compatible with the culture of the area

◆ fairly immediate – it already exists

◆ environmentally friendly – it does little damage, e.g. little pollution.

However, adapting to the conditions has the following disadvantages:

◆ Small scale

◆ Relatively low impact

◆ Not always easy to enforce

◆ Often takes time so a long-term solution

◆ Can make the area more attractive.

When people try to adapt the conditions (e.g. by growing crops in heated greenhouses) problems frequently arise because:

◆ They are ignorant of or choose to ignore local conditions
◆ It takes a lot of resources and technology
◆ It disrupts the existing communities
◆ It damages the existing ecosystems
◆ It is seen as quick and short term.

Prevention/conservation is slower, expensive and complex but does less damage.

Can a world with rapidly growing populations afford to not exploit all environments to the full?

	Manage: The Alps – Alpine convention	Conserve: Antarctica ban
Facts	Area of 192,000km² with 13 million people in 6100 settlements 30,000 animal species and 13,000 plant species Agreement between eight countries in 1991	Area of 14 million km² with 1000 temporary inhabitants in 50 research stations 1000 plant species; mostly algae and lichens Seven countries claim areas but the 1959 Antarctic Treaty is signed by 46 so far
The challenge	◆ Depopulation in some remoter areas ◆ Growth of tourism ◆ Rising 'imported' air pollution (acid rain) ◆ Increased trans-alpine traffic ◆ Global warming impacts	◆ Unexploited minerals – coal, oil, iron ore ◆ Growth of tourism – doubled from 2004 to 2010 (estimated 80,000) ◆ Fishing – 115,000 tonnes a year ◆ Global warming impacts
Attempts at conservation and/or sustainability	◆ Draw up inventory of areas and type of damage ◆ Protect habitats with fences ◆ Restore forests (use jute netting to anchor seedlings) ◆ Reduce traffic – direct to use railways ◆ Soil conservation and restoration of ski slopes ◆ Environmental education and notice boards ◆ Controls on tourist buildings – must harmonise ◆ Water management especially lakes ◆ Encourage traditional farming	◆ Military activities banned ◆ Freedom of scientific research and exchange of information ◆ Nuclear explosions and waste banned ◆ All stations open to inspection ◆ All territorial claims set aside Also, other conventions cover the conservation of fauna and flora (1964), and a ban on mineral exploitation in 1998. Tourism has controlled landing sites and limits on numbers – some areas closed to all activity

Quick check questions

1 Why has there been rapid development of Siberia since the 1990s?

2 Why has tourism only been a recent development in the Antarctic?

3 Why is the Antarctic Treaty increasingly under threat of being broken?

4 How are buildings adapted to minimise their impact on permafrost?

5 Explain why conservation in the Alps had to wait for an agreement between eight countries.

Exam**Café**

Student book pages 88–127

Sample questions

(a) *With the aid of Figure 3 describe the main climatic features in Dawson City (n.b. figure not included). [4 marks]*

▶▶ See page 27.

- 'With the aid of' means you must refer to Figure 3 – you do this by quoting figures, times of year, etc.
- 'Main climatic features' means temperature (max, min and range) and precipitation (total and seasonality).
- It's only four marks so no time or space for non-main features (e.g. wind).
- Do not explain.

(b) *Explain why mass movement is common in cold environments. [6 marks]*

▶▶ See page 2.

- This is 'explain' so don't describe the types of mass movement you know but explanation does differ, e.g. creep versus avalanche.
- 'Common' – in time or space/location.
- Result of waterlogging in summer (heavy and slippery), sludging down permafrost, lack of plants to slow it, weathered material easily saturated, slopes steepened by ice, etc.
- Six marks usually requires two explanatory points well developed.
- Don't forget that labelled diagrams can help.

(c) *In what ways have plants adapted to the conditions in cold environments? [6 marks]*

▶▶ See page 31.

- Six marks usually requires two explanatory points well developed.
- 'Ways' rather than particular plants so look at how leaves, roots, stems, etc, have been adapted and link this to the conditions – climate, soil, drainage, etc.
- Don't forget that labelled diagrams can help.

(d) *With reference to one or more named examples comment on the challenges faced by developments in cold environments. [9 marks]*

▶▶ See page 32.

- This the extended question so there is an expectation of a side of A4.
- One example well chosen is better than several, i.e. depth is more important than variety.
- 'Named examples' means located examples – remember to show evidence of place knowledge by naming places and quoting some details (watch your spelling).
- 'Challenges' is plural so examiners expect more than one challenge. Try to make them different, i.e. not five aspects of climate but climate, permafrost, low population, etc.
- The stress is on challenges, not developments, so you need to list these.
- Best to pick a very challenging one – avoid Taiga, for example.
- You can include diagrams but they must help the discussion, e.g. diagram of active layer in permafrost areas.

Essay questions

Remember: you can't do the cold environment essay in section B if you have done the cold environment question in section A.

With reference to one or more named examples examine how and why cold environments can be exploited for short-term gains. [25 marks]

▶▶ See page 32.

◆ The essay tends (but not always) to come from the later sections of the specification and will normally use wording from the specification, as here.

◆ It is an essay so requires an introduction and conclusion:

Student Answer

Introduction

In Siberia they are drilling for oil and gas in the permafrost area. This is clearly short term as these fossil fuels will be exhausted by 2025. This is happening as the world is short of fuel and Russia wants to use these reserves to develop its economy and political power.

This is fine as far as it goes but where will this lead next as the candidate has answered the question in the introduction? This is a case where more than one example would help develop a more holistic view of development in cold environment. Higher scoring candidates would take a broader view:

Student Answer

Introduction

Cold environments offer a number of possibilities for short-term gain. These partly reflect the nature of the environment, such as fur-trapping or winter sports, but some reflect aspects that are not unique to cold environments such as mineral exploitation, which occur as cold environments have long repelled developers who looked for easier or cheaper conditions first.

◆ Again, 'named examples' means located so the second example above lacked some locational evidence that the first one possessed.

◆ Remember that essays need some structure – this is provided by paragraphs having different aspects. In this case it could be types of short-term developments – hunting/fishing/sealing, minerals/oil, wintersports etc – or it could be different reasons for these developments.

◆ Remember that this is a two-aspect question. Too many candidates ignore (or miss) one of the aspects – **how** and **why**.

◆ How tends to be easier than why – remember that the reasons for development of anywhere could be some inherent attraction or it could be that everywhere else has been used or doesn't want that activity. Hence such remote hostile areas get anti-social or polluting land uses.

◆ A key element here is to question what is 'short term' – it will vary with your viewpoint. Even the idea of 'gains' is debatable – who or what gains? It is this kind of discussion in the conclusion that impresses examiners.

◆ The question carries a negative air about short-term exploitation but try to think where it might be advantageous; e.g. supplying a source of income to support longer-term sustainable development.

Chapter 4 Hot arid and semi-arid environments

Student book pages 132–65

Defining hot arid climates

Hot climates are dry: arid environments have under 250mm rainfall and semi-arid, 250–500mm.

Core climates are:

◆ Hot deserts – e.g. Sahara: winter 13°C, summer 37°C, dry 15mm

◆ Semi-desert – e.g. Kalahari: winter 10°C, summer 23°C, dry 363mm.

Other possible semi-arid environments with distinct periods of aridity:

◆ Savannah – distinct hot dry winters; drought common

◆ Mediterranean – distinct hot dry summers; drought common.

Factors that lead to hot arid climates

Factors are:

◆ latitude – located in subtropical high pressure cells where air is sinking

◆ winds blow outwards – area of trade winds

◆ continentality – at the centre of continents so remote from rain-bearing winds

◆ highland acts as a rain shadow

◆ cold offshore currents – cold air holds less moisture (coastal fog)

◆ human factors – overgrazing of area or excessive water abstraction.

Semi-arid environments have a wet season resulting from the seasonal movement of wind belts.

> **Key words**
>
> Insolation   Radiation
> Continentality

Climatic features

Climatic features are:

◆ prolonged drought – low total rainfall

◆ rainfall in sudden short heavy storms

◆ high day temperatures but very cold nights due to clear skies

◆ low humidity and little cloud

◆ long hours of sunshine

◆ strong winds.

> **Remember**
>
> It is the clear skies that explain the extreme temperature range in deserts.

Processes at work in hot arid environments

Weathering

Mechanical weathering – there is no change in state; material just disintegrates. Mechanical weathering usually occurs as a result of sudden temperature changes between hot days and freezing nights. For instance:

◆ exfoliation – the surface layer flakes off

◆ granular disintegration – light and dark minerals expand/contract at different rates

◆ block disintegration – whole blocks expand and contract

◆ wet/dry (rain also chills the rocks) – clays crack as they shrink on drying

◆ pressure release

◆ hot/cold – rocks can't adjust to very cold nights and sudden hot days

◆ freeze-thaw – usually in high areas

◆ hydration – rocks absorb water and expand

◆ crystal growth – salt crystals grow in weaknesses in the rock.

Chemical weathering – there is no change in state; material just decomposes. Chemical weathering usually happens following rare rain or fog. For instance:

- solution – especially of iron or salt-rich rocks
- acid action – carbonic acid dissolves lime-rich rocks
- oxidation – rusting.

Biological weathering – weathering by plants, e.g. roots and animals (usually in a search for water).

Wind

Why is wind so effective in arid environments?

- Extreme pressure differences – deserts are areas where the air above sinks to form intense high pressure areas; also, heated air rises rapidly
- Little vegetation to slow wind
- A lot of arid areas are level (e.g. salt pans), so there is little to slow the wind
- A lot of fine debris (sand) from mechanical weathering.

Wind erodes by:

- corrasion – wind-blown sand erodes rocks
- attrition – particles collide and wear each other smaller
- deflation – wind picks up and moves loose material.

Wind transports by:

- suspension – fine sediment carried within the air
- saltation – usually sand grains hopping along the surface
- surface creep – rolling along the ground.

Water

Why is water a major factor in arid environments?

- Flash floods – rare thunderstorms but ground is baked so runoff is rapid
- Exogenous rivers – flow from wetter areas
- Historic water – at the end of the last ice age, these climates were wetter
- Underground water – groundwater
- Fog may bring moisture to these arid areas.

Quick check questions

1. What is the main reason why hot arid areas are so common in the tropics?
2. Why are nights so cold in hot arid areas?
3. Why are winds so strong in hot arid areas?
4. How does the wind erode rocks?
5. What is an 'exogenous river'?

Features of hot arid areas

Student book pages 142–49

You should be able to **describe** features of hot arid areas, i.e. their shape, size, location, composition and **explain** how they were formed. The most effective way is with well-annotated diagrams.

Features result from:

◆ **E**rosion – wind action (deflation hollows or sculptured rocks such as gour, yardangs and zeugens) flash floods (or historical – wadi, gullies, pediment) and exotic rivers (canyon)

◆ **T**ransport – mass movement (creep, slides) flash floods, wind

◆ **D**eposition – wind (ripples, ridges, barchan dune, seif dune), flash floods (fans, bahada, playa).

Key words

Exogenous river	Pediment
Playa	

Most questions ask you to describe and explain two features resulting from water and wind:

Water features

Canyons

Wadis

Salt pans

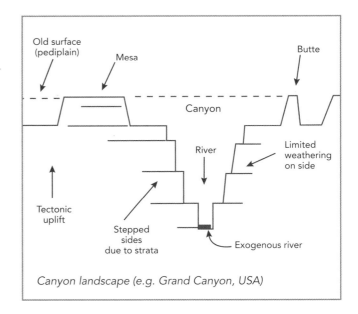

Canyon landscape (e.g. Grand Canyon, USA)

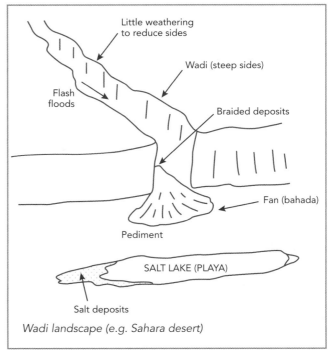

Wadi landscape (e.g. Sahara desert)

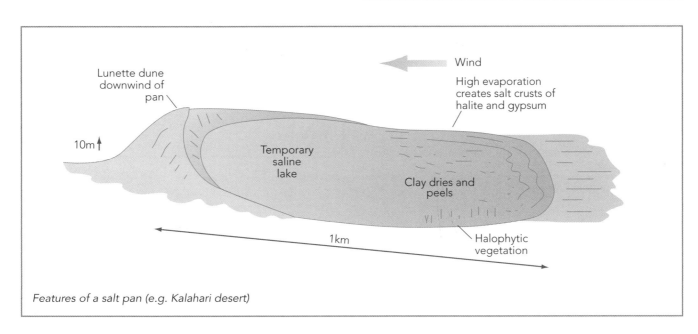

Features of a salt pan (e.g. Kalahari desert)

Wind features

Sand dunes

Sculptured rocks

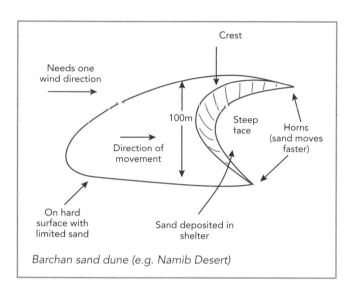

Barchan sand dune (e.g. Namib Desert)

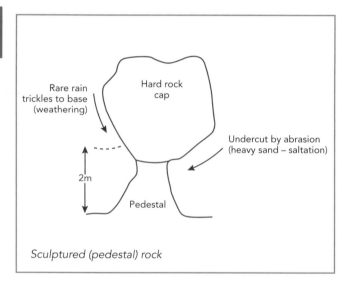

Sculptured (pedestal) rock

Quick check questions

1   Why do flash floods occur in hot arid areas?

2   Why might it be dangerous to travel along a wadi?

3   Why do salt pans form around lakes in hot arid areas?

4   Do all hot arid areas have sand dunes? Explain your answer.

5   Why are wind-sculptured rocks usually undercut in hot arid areas?

Impact of climate on the ecosystem

Student book pages 149–52

Plants and animals have to adapt to:

◆   prolonged drought – the Atacama Desert, Chile has never recorded rain

◆   very cold nights – below feezing as clear skies so rapid heat loss

◆   very hot days

◆   strong erosive winds including sand storms

◆   soft sand or hard rock – little if any soil

◆   high salt content of water due to high evaporation

◆   competition for water and scarce nutrients

◆   large number and variety of consumers.

Plants adapt by:

◆   size – tend to be small and sparse

◆   roots – either shallow to grab what rain there is or deep to find underground water

◆   stems – store water, e.g. cacti, thick walled to reduce water loss

◆   leaves – small and waxy or thorns to reduce surface water loss and protect plant. Leaves may die off in dry season

◆   life cycle – remain as seeds until rains come (then a rapid life cycle and the desert blooms).

◆   reproduction – often very bright flowers to attract the few pollinators. Use wind or animals (burrs or sticky seeds) to spread their seeds

◆   other means – some excrete toxins to protect themselves, e.g. creosote bush.

Key words

Xerophytic   Ephermerals

Halophytic

Animals adapt by:

- size – small to reduce water loss and maximise heat loss, e.g. gerbil
- habit – nocturnal, hibernate in dry season or burrow
- bodies – store water in bloodstream and food as fat with a thick skin to reduce water loss and protect against sand
- feet – padded to protect from hot sand
- heads – often large ears for cooling, second eyelids to keep out sand, camel can close nostrils to keep out sand
- waste disposal – concentrate urine and faeces to reduce water loss
- food – many are omnivores as food is scarce: tough stomach to digest thorn scrub
- life cycle – rapid following rains, often numerous offspring
- colour – light to reflect heat and blend into the background sand/dust, e.g. camel, fennec fox.

Key words

| Net primary productivity | Omnivore |
| Food pyramid | Scavenger |

Exam tips

The environment may not be so fragile as it has adapted to harsh conditions for so long. It is much harder to wipe out such tough resilient vegetation (very like weeds).

Why so fragile?

Student book pages 153–54

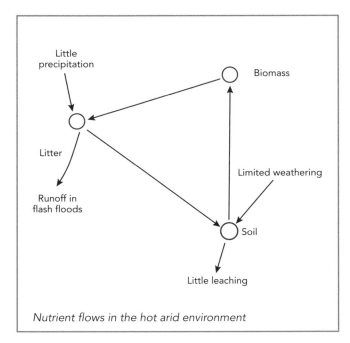

Nutrient flows in the hot arid environment

Why may the hot and semi-arid environment be fragile?

- Extreme climate with 'sudden' events, e.g. sand storms, thunderstorms, fires
- Delicate nature of water supply (surface and subsurface)
- Low-energy environment (low inputs – dry but high sun energy)
- Low nutrient stores, vulnerable flows – fierce competition
- Limited range of species – limited gene pool and short food chains
- Traditionally low density self-sufficient human population.

Case study: Mojave Desert, USA

Student book pages 153–54

	Examples
Natural threats	
Climatic	Cold winters have killed saguaro cacti
Competition	From new species; e.g. wild donkeys and buffle grass
Fire	1994 – 1150 acres of land were on fire. Saguaro vulnerable to fire
Human threats	
Urbanisation	Growth of cities such as Phoenix
Transport	Roads and pipelines restrict movement of animals
Industry	New high-tech industry attracted by aridity but noise and traffic scare animals and clear vegetation
Recreation	Off-road vehicles crush plants; golf courses; disturbance of the ecosystem
Mining	Prospecting and mining disturb wildlife
Farming	Overgrazing by sheep, goats and cattle and compacting the soil. Also, irrigation increases the build-up of salts in soil
Other	People remove cacti and tortoises for their gardens

Quick check questions

1 Why do plants in hot arid areas have small leaves?

2 What is the advantage to animals in having large ears in hot arid areas?

3 What is 'Desert Bloom'?

4 Why are so many creatures nocturnal in hot arid areas?

5 Why do so many people in MEDCs want to live in hot arid areas?

Opportunities and challenges

Student book pages 155–62

Opportunities

The opportunities provided by hot and arid environments include:

◆ power production – wind, solar

◆ industry – tourism because hot and sunny, hi-tech industry as dry, e.g. USA film-making

◆ settlement – military bases, resorts, e.g. Las Vegas

◆ mining – oil, gas, ores (exposed as little vegetation and few objects to go into waste tips)

◆ agriculture – grazing, irrigated farming or early crops under polythene

◆ waste disposal – as few object

◆ military – used for testing, e.g. Nevada nuclear tests, Woomera in Australia missile testing.

Remember

Opportunities may change as society and technology change, e.g. golf courses in the desert in Arizona and Dubai.

Key words

Pastoralists	Conservation
Eco-tourist	National Park

Case studies: Thar desert and Australia deserts

Student book pages 160–63

1. Resources

	Thar desert: agriculture	Australia deserts: minerals
Facts	200,000 km² but densely populated area along India/Pakistan border	Vast range of mineral ores – uranium, gold, copper, opals, iron ore
Environmental impacts	◆ Vast goat and sheep herds have overgrazed the area causing soil erosion ◆ Trees and shrubs removed for fuel and building ◆ Virtual monoculture of millet leaves soil exhausted ◆ Excessive irrigation has caused water logging and salinisation ◆ Waterlogging has increased malaria ◆ Loss of local habitats	◆ Mining uses vast quantities of water – extract underground artesian water ◆ Construction of roads, rail pipelines and facilities damages habitats ◆ Waste disposal problems – leaks from processing pollute soil and water ◆ Eyesore, e.g. much is open cast – copper mine 1km wide with spoil heaps
Economic impacts	◆ Creates jobs ◆ Cash crops of rice and sugar cane have raised local incomes ◆ High cost of irrigation, e.g. Rajasthan canal is 650km long	◆ Creates jobs, e.g. copper mine at Olympic dam employs 3000 ◆ Tax revenue ◆ Improved local infrastructure and services ◆ Cost of importing food and materials to area
Social impacts	◆ Increased population growth in this marginal area	◆ Increased house prices so locals can't afford them ◆ Influx of foreign workers – gender imbalance ◆ Problems over drinking and violence
Political impacts	◆ Disputes over use of the headwaters (in India) of the Indus (in Pakistan) for irrigation	◆ Some local aboriginals dispute mineral rights ◆ Who should own these rights – state versus nation
Cultural impacts	◆ Traditional way of life lost ◆ Pastoralists being settled and herds reduced	◆ Aboriginals have lost links to their land ◆ Destruction of sacred places ◆ Influx of new more westernised workers and cultures

Student book pages 157–58

	Valley of the Kings, Egypt	Grand Canyon, USA
Facts	Been a tourist attraction since Roman times. Gets 5 million visitors a year. Two valleys and over 60 tombs	National Park created in 1919. 500,000 hectares and has 450km of the canyon. Gets 5 million visitors a year
Environmental impacts	◆ Visitors' breath increases humidity in tombs so damaging murals, etc ◆ Air pollution from tour buses ◆ Hotels use scarce water – hotel pools suffer evaporation loss ◆ Overcrowding	◆ Minimal as access tightly controlled with limited roads and hotels ◆ Permits needed for fishing, camping etc ◆ Much is kept inaccessible to protect habitats ◆ Helicopter flights rationed
Economic impacts	◆ Increased entry fees to limit numbers ◆ Increased employment – guides, local souvenir industries ◆ Improved infrastructure – roads, water, power, etc ◆ Earns lot of foreign exchange (Egypt earns 45% of exports from tourism) ◆ Money used to restore tombs ◆ Hotel construction	◆ Local airport but limited infrastructure ◆ Some employment, e.g. guides, park rangers
Social impacts	◆ Westernised tourists clash with Muslim locals, e.g. over females in shorts ◆ Great disparity in wealth between locals and tourists ◆ Increased crime	◆ Limited as National Park so kept as wilderness ◆ Some impact on local Native Americans
Political impacts	◆ 58 tourists killed by extremists in 1997 ◆ Source of resentment to fundamentalist nationalists	◆ National Park so is state owned but on land claimed by the Hualapai Native Americans

Remember

The very aridity attracts some activities such as film-making, aircraft storage and military testing.

Challenges

The challenges of hot and arid environments can be categorised as physical and human factors.

Physical factors include:

◆ climate – harsh and extreme (dust storms)

◆ relief – shifting sands, steep slopes, jagged rocks

◆ vegetation – thin and tough

◆ drainage – lack of water

◆ ecosystem – hostile, e.g. snakes or low productivity

◆ soils – extremely thin and alkaline (salts) or salty.

Human factors include:

◆ high-cost environment (water, cooling)

◆ remote and land transport difficult

◆ pollution threats, e.g. oil

◆ waste disposal

◆ existing indigenous populations – usually nomadic

◆ need for conservation but few care as there is a low population.

How can hot arid areas be managed sustainably?

Student book pages 159–62

Key words

Sustainability

Nomadism

Intermediate technology

Desertification

Management challenges

Management challenges involve how to balance the environmental needs (e.g. wildlife, hydrology and vegetation) against economic factors (e.g. farming, employment and transport) and social factors (e.g. stark scenery and historic/cultural aspects).

Issues

The following issues need to be considered when managing hot arid and semi-arid environments:

◆ What is the exact nature of the environmental and water resources and their status (quality versus quantity)?

◆ Sheer cost – short versus long term, e.g. the Central Arizona water transfer cost $50 billion in the 1990s. Who should pay? Local versus national issue – rate payer (or water board) versus tax payer.

◆ Who pays versus who gains? Should tax payers subsidise developments that benefit a small group, e.g. farmers? The death of the lower Rio Grande well exemplifies this. How effective is the scheme and for whom?

◆ Political will, e.g. the Sahara Desert is occupied by at least 13 countries. Ownership – who is responsible for rivers flowing through deserts? E.g. the Niger starts in Guinea but flows through Mali, Niger and Nigeria.

◆ Technology – has the area the knowledge and expertise to develop the challenging environment? Is enough known about that particular environment?

◆ Size or scale – definition of the area that makes up the project area. It is easier to manage smaller areas, e.g. Sahara covers 85 per cent of North Africa.

◆ How long will it take? Quick fix versus long term, e.g. desertification is increasing partly as a result of global warming.

◆ Wider impacts. What implications are there for areas beyond the project area, e.g. irrigation on the upper Niger has a big impact on Sahelian countries?

Approaches

There are two approaches to managing hot and semi-arid environments: low-tech and hi-tech. A low-tech approach uses simple or traditional techniques often 'borrowed' from other similar climatic areas, e.g. drought resistant trees from Australia.

A low-tech approach is:

◆ cheap

◆ easily understood and needs little skill/education

◆ compatible with culture

◆ labour intensive

◆ fairly immediate

◆ environmentally friendly

but it is also:

◆ small scale

◆ time taking

◆ relatively low impact.

Exam tips

This is a good example of the determinism versus possibilities concepts, which would be impressive to mention in an extended answer.

Remember

Desert borders are often straight lines as they were drawn up by colonial powers who disregarded the local nomadic populations.

Exam tips

It is always good to see some contrast in approaches to problems – there is not only one way of viewing them.

	Sahel, Niger **Student book page 162**	Arizona
Facts	Life expectancy 44 years GNP is $900 per capita Population growth of 2.9%	Life expectancy 78 years GNP $28,000 per capita Population growth of 6%
The challenges	◆ Desertification ◆ Land ruined by excessive irrigation causing saline crusts ◆ Overgrazing by goats ◆ Recurring droughts ◆ Locusts in 1995	◆ Fastest growing state – retirement ◆ Excessive use of groundwater ◆ Entitled to 50% of water of Colorado River (rest to California)
Short-term gains	◆ Growth in livestock for export ◆ Uranium and gold mining ◆ Oil exploitation	◆ Cotton cash cropping ◆ Copper mining ◆ Tourism – e.g. Grand Canyon
Attempts at sustainability	◆ Use mulches to improve soil and add moisture ◆ Planting pits – collect any runoff ◆ Intercropping – shrubs between millet rows to reduce wind damage ◆ Bunds – low stone walls along the contours to hold top soil and water ◆ Use of dung to retain moisture in soil ◆ Growing drought-resistant crop varieties ◆ Planting drought-resistant trees	◆ Vast dams on Colorado – Lakes Mead and Powell ◆ Water transfer schemes to Phoenix and Tucson ◆ Water farming – buying land for its water store But now: ◆ Precision levelling to conserve irrigation water ◆ Remote sensing (Agiis) to ensure exact needs of crops are met so saving water ◆ New irrigation techniques such as buried drip and precision sprinklers

Quick check questions

1 What is the main reason for the fall in crop yields in the irrigated areas of the Thar desert?

2 Why are international borders so straight in desert areas? Why does this cause problems?

3 Why is a nomadic lifestyle difficult in hot arid areas today?

4 What is the main problem caused by tourism in hot arid areas?

5 Why are low-tech traditional solutions to aridity more effective than big projects?

Sample questions

1 *The sample questions will tend to be worded in a similar way as the questions for the cold environment – they are seen as pairs as you can't do both.*

(a) With the aid of Figure 4, describe the location of hot arid areas (n.b. figure not included). [4 marks]

◆ 'With the aid of' means you must refer to Figure 4 – you do this by quoting locations, e.g. latitude, distance from coast and directions.
◆ 'Location' means where they are – look for patterns or common features, e.g. in the tropics.
◆ It's only four marks so aim for four clear locational aspects.
◆ Do not explain.

(b) Explain why water has an important role in forming landforms in hot arid environments. [6 marks]

▶▶ See page 40.

◆ This is 'explain' so don't describe the types of landforms you know. Explanation should contain distinctly different points, e.g. thunderstorms versus historical water.
◆ 'Important' – in time, space/location or speed.
◆ Don't forget landforms under groundwater.
◆ Six marks usually requires two well-developed explanatory points. If you do two, make them a contrast.
◆ Don't forget that labelled diagrams can help but are unlikely to be useful here.

(c) In what ways are ecosystems in hot arid environments considered fragile? [6 marks]

▶▶ See page 43.

◆ Six marks usually requires two well-developed explanatory points.
◆ 'Ways' refers to broad principles such as the vulnerability of food chains to extreme conditions; not a list of how each animal or plant is fragile.
◆ Don't forget that labelled diagrams can help – here one to show the size of nutrient flows and stores would be useful.

(d) With reference to one or more named examples, comment on the opportunities for economic developments in hot arid environments. [9 marks]

▶▶ See page 44.

◆ This is the extended question so there is an expectation of a side of A4.
◆ One example well chosen is better than several, i.e. depth is more important than variety.
◆ 'Named examples' means located examples – remember to show evidence of place knowledge by naming places and quoting some details (watch your spelling).

- ‘Opportunities’ has an ‘s’ so examiners expect more than one opportunity. Try to use an example that gives more than one opportunity and make them different, i.e. not five aspects of tourism but tourism, farming, residential, etc.
- ‘Comment’ suggests you try to link these opportunities to hot arid conditions (show clear cause–effect).
- Most likely, this is best exemplified from MEDC.
- You can include maps or diagrams but they must help the discussion, e.g. map of Central Arizona Plan features.

Essay questions

Remember: you can't do the hot arid environment essay in section B if you have done the hot arid environment question in section A.

With reference to one or more named examples, examine how careful management helps to ensure sustainability in hot arid environments. [25 marks]

▶▶ See page 47.
- The essay tends (but not always) to come from the later sections of the specification and will normally use wording from the specification as here.
- It is an essay so requires an introduction and conclusion. Conclusions are crucial and should re-visit the question title to summarise the thrust of the preceding discussion.

Student Answer

Careful management can at best improve the level of sustainability in such fragile areas. Most schemes seek to manage water sources and limit pollution as in the Mojave Desert, which is part of a state-owned National Park. Elsewhere it is not easy to be sustainable as often this costs money, reduces returns and is too easily disturbed by adjacent areas where there is no such management. As hot arid areas are often seen as wastelands many do not recognise them as worth preserving or protecting and rather see them as ideal areas for anti-social activities such as nuclear testing.

This is quite effective as a conclusion. It questions the concept of sustainability and suggests that where such areas are privately owned, different values and attitudes may influence the type and effectiveness of environmental management. A further refinement would have been to point out that the concept of sustainability is a long-term one and that this might differ with your viewpoint – an environmentalist may have very different ideas of sustainability from those of a farmer.

- Again, ‘named examples’ means located so the example above needed a little more clarity over location. Too many candidates assume examiners know where examples are – in this case ‘south-west USA’ would have helped.
- Remember that essays need some structure – this is provided by paragraphs having different aspects. In this case it could be scales of management (e.g. local, district, regional) or by type (e.g. National Park, irrigation project).
- A key element here is to question what is ‘helps to ensure’ – it will vary with your viewpoint. Even the idea of ‘helps’ is debatable – could management make things worse? It is this kind of discussion in the conclusion that impresses examiners.

Chapter 5
Managing urban change

Student book pages 172–209

Characteristics of urban areas

Student book pages 174–85

Functions

Functions of urban areas include residential, services, commercial, industrial, tourism, cultural, administrative, political, entertainment, recreational and transport.

Features

Urban areas have the following features:

◆ **environmental** – buildings, pollution, little natural environment
◆ **economic** – employment in secondary and tertiary industry, commerce dominates
◆ **social** – high population density, socio-economic diversity, urban culture.

Key words

City	Mega-city
Conurbation	Primate city

Land-use patterns

Land-use patterns are:

a) Concentric rings
b) Sectors or wedges
c) Multi-nuclei or blocks
d) Combinations of above
e) Chaotic or unplanned

Exam tips

Questions often ask you to describe patterns of land use – try to use these terms.

Factors that influence land-use patterns

Student book page 179

Key words

Site	Inertia
Situation	

The following factors influence patterns of land use:

◆ Physical site – climate, relief, drainage, rock type
◆ Economic factors:
   – Transport routes and accessibility (sectors – Hoyt)
   – Ability to outbid for sites (Burgess)
   – Size of site available
   – Mutual attraction/repulsion (Harris and Ullman)
   – Income
◆ Social:
   – Life cycle
   – Tenure – who controls the land/buildings
   – Historical – inertia, conservation, reputation
   – Mobility of population
   – Mutual attraction/repulsion
   – Land ownership – estate development
   – Ethnicity and cultural factors – spatial segregation
   – Religious factors – attraction
◆ Political:
   – planning controls – land-use zoning, green belt
   – need for centrality or safety (defence)
   – state or authority boundaries.

Exam tips

Some of these factors can be seen on a map – especially the physical factors, which often caused the initial pattern. Remember: most European urban areas were initiated in pre-industrial times when physical factors dominated.

Factors related to land-use patterns

	Concentric	Sectors	Multi-nuclei
Physical	Uniform area	Along rivers, coasts Along mineral outcrops	Diverse area, e.g. hills
Economic	Bid-rent	Transport routes	Repulsion Attraction
Social	Family status Age	Economic status	Ethnicity
Political	Defensive site	Border	Planning Land-use zoning
Historical	Pre-industrial	Industrial period	Current

Urban processes

> **Student book pages 180–82**

Urban processes are external and internal.

External processes affect the whole urban area:

◆ Urbanisation – movement into cities

◆ Counterurbanisation – movement out of cities

◆ Agglomeration – grouping together of functions etc

◆ Suburbanisation – movement to urban fringe.

Internal processes occur within an area or zone:

◆ Regeneration – the renewal of an area

◆ Gentrification – area attracts the more wealthy

◆ Re-imaging – changing the image or reputation of an area

◆ Filtering – certain groups move out leaving others behind

◆ Exclusion – shutting out of particular community groups.

Case study: two urban areas

> **Student book pages 182–84**

	MEDC – Newcastle, UK 190,000 people	LEDC – Lagos, Nigeria 8 million people
Land-use pattern and planned nuclei	Broadly concentric but sector of old industry and docks along River Tyne	Originally around three islands but now large sector growth along highways and railway
Physical	River – limited north–south crossings but provided water and port	Three islands with river access to interior and gap in coastal reefs Cooler coastal breezes
Economic	Was heavy industry based on local coal and ship building along Tyne. Now, assembly industries, commerce, retail and entertainment. Very much seen as regional centre for north-east	Important export port Main industrial centre based on imports and processing local crops Main office and commercial centre On end of three trans-African highways and railway
Social	Some sorting by socio-economic group (via public housing, e.g. Byker) and ethnicity	Some sorting by socio-economic group (via shanty towns on fringes and ex-colonial areas such as Victoria) and ethnicity (tribal or village transplants)
Political	Border town Defensive site – castle	Main British base in western Africa Defensive site – forts
Historical	Originally Roman settlement at end of Hadrian's Wall (Wallsend) Later Norman centre to control the north	Originally slave port for local tribe then taken over by Portugal and then Britain in 1861. Capital up to 1991
Processes	Counterurbanisation Suburbanisation Regeneration Filtering Gentrification	Urbanisation Agglomeration Suburbanisation Exclusion Rural–urban migration

Urban change – causes/ issues

Student book pages 185–94

Causes of change

The following factors cause urban change:

◆ Population change – migration in/out, birth rate, ethnic mix, age structure

◆ Mobility change – increased private and public transport

◆ Technology change – different locational factors are now important, change in range and cost of transport

◆ Perceptions change – residential preference, perception of safety, crime, etc

◆ Incomes and wealth change – increased or decreased

◆ Political strategies change – planning initiatives, local tax changes, land use zoning

◆ Employment structure/location change – industrial versus services growth or decline, changing technology

◆ Public services demand and supply change – type, location.

Issues resulting from change

Exam tips

Remember these can apply to both LEDC and MEDC urban areas but the nature of the issues will probably vary.

Physical issues:

◆ Climate – creation of urban micro-climate

◆ Relief – building on unsuitable sites, e.g. steep slope

◆ Drainage – lack of, water shortage, water pollution, flash floods

◆ Vegetation – loss of habitats

◆ Pollution – air (e.g. smog), water, land, noise, visual, thermal

◆ Increased risk of extreme events, e.g. floods, landslides.

Economic issues:

◆ Power – shortage, reliability, cost

◆ Industry – lack of jobs or low pay, exploitation, informal economy

◆ Settlement – housing quality and quantity, cost, tenure

◆ Property prices – housing tenure

◆ Cost of living – prices, choice of products and services

◆ Services – lack of sufficient schools, clinics, etc

◆ Transport – congestion, poor public transport

◆ Local tax base – compared to demands on public sector services

◆ Implication for surrounding rural areas (e.g. as food suppliers).

Social issues:

◆ Wealth inequality and deprivation – will probably increase, cycle of poverty

◆ Ethnic tensions, prejudice, discrimination, clash of cultures

◆ High cost of social support – overstretched, post code rationing

◆ Inner city decay

◆ Slums and shanties

◆ Crime and security issues – vandalism, theft, violence, cost of police

◆ Pace of life – stress, nervous breakdowns, family breakdowns.

Political issues:

◆ Voting patterns

◆ Polarisation.

	Growth in Dhaka	Decline in Birmingham
	Grown five times in last 20 years 7 million people	Population fell 9% 1991–2001 1 million people
Physical	Pollution (especially air and water) increasing – disease common	Derelict land and brownfield sites Air and water pollution decreasing
Economic	Growth in manufacturing (TNCs) Growth in services Increased congestion Shanty housing (bostis)	Decline of manufacturing Growth of services Increased congestion Empty housing
Social	High unemployment Lack of services Large informal economy Majority below poverty line Religious tension Village transplants	High unemployment Services closing, e.g. schools Deprivation increases Exclusion Ethnic tension Family break-up
Political	Strong polarisation of rich and poor Lack of rate revenue as so many poor	Strong polarisation Lack of rate revenue as wealthy move out

Socio-economic deprivation

Deprivation is when a person's well-being falls below a level generally regarded as an acceptable minimum.

Poverty is found in a variety of locations:

- Poverty clusters in inner-city areas, ex-industrial areas, e.g. Hulme in Manchester
- Persistent areas of poverty, e.g. East End of London
- Marginal land – on steep slopes or areas prone to flooding, e.g. shanty towns in Rio de Janeiro
- Fringe areas – peripheral estates often have public housing, e.g. Glasgow.

Key words

Multiple deprivation	Ghetto
Ethnoburb	Gentrification

Poverty is often seen as including:

- fuel poverty – can't afford to keep warm
- service poverty – have little access to services (private and public)
- financial exclusion – financial institutions limit support
- digital divide – lack access to ICT and the Internet
- powerlessness – lack political influence.

Exam tips

The term poverty is very complex and should be seen as a relative term. Some see it as relative to the standard of living; others to the possession of the basic necessities of life.

Groups that are most prone to poverty include:

- Elderly people – pensions are low and rarely keep up with inflation
- Ethnic minorities – often suffer discrimination so have low-paid jobs
- Unemployed people – especially if long term due to illness or disability
- Single parents with young families – unlikely to be able to work and can't afford child care.

Socio-economic differences

These result from the polarisation of groups – like attracts like. Also, it reflects the role of house prices in restricting access to certain areas.

There are negative forces which tend to force groups out of areas:

- High house prices
- Discrimination in employment
- Perceived threat of violence.

There are also positive forces which tend to attract groups to areas:

- Social contacts, e.g. family, friends
- Cultural practices, e.g. religion, schools, entertainment
- Service provision, e.g. special shops, finance.

Exam tips

New towns in Britain were originally planned as areas of mixed socio-economic groups but today the groups have separated out, illustrating this tendency to polarise.

Managing growth in demand for services

Student book page 192

Services include public services such as health, education, libraries and care homes.

Demand for services is exceeding supply.

Rising demand is due to:
- an ageing population
- more urban poor
- increased expectations
- ever smaller family units – high divorce rates
- increased mental health issues and stress.

Falling or limited supply is due to:
- increased cost of providing services (technology, transport, labour costs, etc)
- reduced funding (less income from local taxes, etc)
- widening types of demand – can't meet them all
- danger of creating a dependency culture.

As a result, a vicious circle is created:

The vicious circle of urban decay

Strategies used to manage socio-economic issues

1) **Bottom up:**
- Self-help schemes, e.g. Assisted Self Help (ASH) in Rio de Janeiro shanty towns
- Co-operative schemes, e.g. housing associations, credit schemes
- Improved education and hence economic mobility.

2) **Top down:**
- Refurbishment, e.g. Glasgow Eastern Area Renewal (GEAR) project in 1976–87
- Urban redevelopment or renewal, e.g. London Docklands Development Corporation (LDDC) of 1980s
- Urban regeneration, e.g. Neighbourhood Renewal Fund 2001–06
- Wider policies such as taxation, social security, etc.

Exam tips

Bottom-up schemes face real problems as they lack sufficient funds to make a change big enough to be self-generating. Socially they are ideal but economically they face problems.

Quick check questions

1 Why is 'poverty' a relative term?

2 Explain what is meant by the term 'financial exclusion'.

3 What is the main mechanism that limits access to housing in a particular area?

4 Why is urban tax income falling in most MEDC large urban areas?

5 What do the initials ASH stand for in LEDC housing development?

Case study: shanty towns (favelas, barridas, townships, etc)

	Slums of hope?	Slums of despair?
Housing	Can build to own design Can expand as needed Cheap to build – scrap material Rent free	Often unsafe and prone to fire Lack of space – no open space No foundations so collapse Don't own the land so can be forced off Often on unsafe marginal land
Infrastructure	Poor but often link illegally to power grid No tarmac roads but no cars	Lack of services Fires are common as people cook on fires
Sanitation	Lot of recycling – night soil for rural areas or urban farms	Lack leads to disease and epidemics. High infant death rate
Jobs	Large 'black' or informal economy Flexible – easily adjust to changing demand for labour	Lack of permanent jobs No job security Low pay, no pensions Child labour is common
Education	Community generated – linked to needs Often listen to elders	Outside state system so few formal qualifications Often traditional content
Safety	Community polices itself	Police and security keep out so easily exploited. High murder and crime rates
Community	Often strong sense of community Migration is usually from same village or to a relative Run own affairs Can avoid taxation, national service, etc Can 'hide' from responsibilities, e.g. arranged marriage	Dominated by 'men of violence' Ignored by government as have no right to vote Self interest overrules community spirit No legal rights

Solutions to the shanty town problem

	Advantages	Disadvantages
Assisted Self Help (ASH), e.g. Rochina in Brazil	Cheap Quick as simple Low technology Creates local jobs Maintains community spirit	Money is spread thin Can take time as small scale Keeps housing poor standard Lack skills or are temporary Can divide the community
Slum clearance, e.g. Harare in Zimbabwe	Quick Removes eyesore Reduces source of crime, etc Restores legal land ownership	Causes massive resistance Simply moves problem elsewhere May rebuild back on same land Corruption
High-density public housing, e.g. Hong Kong	Quality housing Security of tenure Has infrastructure so less disease, etc Structurally safer	Increased rents Often rules, e.g. no pets Cost of services Lower density than slums so re-housing needed May attract more to migrate in Increases birth rate
New towns, e.g. Cairo	Quality housing Spreads problem elsewhere Creates jobs Improves infrastructure	Increased rent People don't want to live there Lack of jobs High cost
Reverse rural to urban migration, e.g. Brazil	Develops interior rural areas Reduces pressure on city Low cost to city Return to own culture	Can damage environment Moves the problem elsewhere High cost to rural area People don't want to live there Few rural jobs

Environmental issues

Student book pages 194–202

The following environmental issues occur in urban areas:

- Pollution – air, water, noise, visual, solids, light
- Water – scarcity (transfer schemes, use of aquifers, reservoir building)
- Traffic – congestion, pollution, land use (roads, car parks, garages, etc)
- Land – pressure on marginal land and ecosystems (parks, conservation, green belts)
- Micro-climate – heat island, wind channelling, higher rainfall, smog
- Dereliction – visual pollution, safety, health.

Traffic congestion (e.g. London)

Student book page 202

Causes:

- Rise in private car ownership
- Increased dispersal of employment and services (e.g. shops)
- Decline in public transport
- Increased complexity of traffic mix (e.g. lorries)
- Outdated and inadequate road patterns (often radial).

Exam tips

Remember: many of these causes (and problems) are linked and it is not always easy to sort out which caused which.

Problems that result:

- Wastes time especially at peak times
- Cost of fuel and increased fuel consumption
- Increased air pollution
- Increased noise
- Driver stress – increased accidents
- Cost of damage to roads, etc
- Space taken up by roads, parking, garages, etc.

Management:

- Penalise car users, e.g. congestion charges, increased tax, bans (odd/even number plates), higher fuel prices

- Improved traffic management – traffic lights, roundabouts, speed restrictions
- Improved road systems – flyovers, tunnels, by-passes, ring roads
- Parking controls – park and ride schemes, permits, charging
- Improve non-car options – e.g. cycle paths, walking, bus
- Improve vehicle technology – electric cars (LEV and ZEV)
- Improve public transport – low prices, bus-lanes, tram systems, mass transit
- Traffic information systems – plot quicker routes
- Non-transport options – e.g. teleworking, flexi-hours, compaction of cities.

Key words

LEV = low emission vehicle	Congestion charging
ZEV = zero emission vehicle	Pedestrian precinct

Increasing volumes of waste (e.g. Mumbai)

Student book page 202

Causes:

- Increased packaging – branding, advertising
- Westernised 'throw away societies' – litter
- Poor collection services, e.g. LEDCs
- Increased population.

Problems:

- Landfill sites being filled, create methane (global warming), leach into groundwater
- Cost of collection
- Vermin increase – rats, insects
- Smell and visual pollution
- Risk of disease outbreak.

Management:

- Recycling and sorting of waste
- Re-using materials
- Incineration – generate electricity (danger of dioxins)
- Charging for waste disposal
- Controls or taxes on packaging
- Find new disposal sites in LEDCs.

Pollution (air, water, noise, light, visual, thermal)

Causes:

◆ Traffic congestion

◆ Urban canyons – buildings trap fumes, heat, etc

◆ Domestic and commercial heating and cooling

◆ Buildings give off heat, light

◆ Increased urban population.

Problems:

◆ Increased diseases – asthma, bronchitis, cancer

◆ Acid rain – damage to buildings

◆ Creation of urban micro-climate

◆ Smog and photochemical smog

◆ Lost days at work

◆ Cost of cleaning buildings, etc

◆ Lower sunshine hours cause depression.

Management:

◆ Laws – e.g. Clean Air Act

◆ Inspection and maintenance checks on vehicles, etc

◆ Movement of sources, e.g. heavy industry to LEDCs

◆ Technology = more recycling of water, air or reusing, e.g. waste water for watering plants.

Growth of urban areas

Student book pages 199–200

Causes:

◆ Improved transport/roads so longer commuting is possible

◆ People living at lower density, e.g. smaller family units

◆ Ageing population – want to be near urban services

◆ Increased urban population

◆ Building of speculative estates ahead of demand

◆ Green belts – developers 'jump' the belt

◆ Development of more urban fringe activities, e.g. recreation

◆ Suburbanisation – in the USA this was called 'white flight'.

	Push from inner zones	Pull to suburbs
Physical	Pollution Little open space/ gardens Congestion	Fresh country air More open space/ gardens Easier accessibility
Economic	High rents and prices High rates and taxes Parking problems	Lower house prices More employment Space for parking
Social	Fear of crime and violence Older ageing property Influx of migrants Overstretched services	Safer neighbourhoods Newer larger houses Mix with similar people Better schools and services
Political	Extremist politics Fear of unrest	Moderate politics

Problems:

◆ Building on floodplains means an increased flood risk

◆ Building on unstable slopes can cause landslides

◆ Loss of habitats, e.g. wetlands

◆ Loss of farmland and open space, e.g. woodlands

◆ Absorption of surrounding villages and towns.

Management:

◆ Restrict outward growth, e.g. green belt policy, land-use zoning

◆ Deflect growth to planned centres, e.g. new town policy

◆ Increase urban density – more vertical building (compaction)

◆ Re-develop derelict or brownfield land.

Urban dereliction

Causes:

◆ Simple ageing of buildings with time

◆ Maintenance costs exceed income from property

◆ Movement out of urban activities to fringe locations (cheaper and more accessible)

◆ Building design doesn't suit modern uses, e.g. open plan offices

◆ Decreased access by transport (due to increase in lorry size)

◆ Changes in technology – both building technology and process technology.

Problems:

◆ Derelict buildings and land

◆ Visual pollution

◆ Increased vandalism, damage, fires, etc

◆ Increased risk to health and safety (e.g. building collapse)

◆ Contaminated sites – toxic residues.

Case studies: management

Student book page 202

	London – MEDC	Mumbai – LEDC/NIC
	Population 8.5m, density 4800 people per km^2 Area 1600km^2	Population 18m, density 29,000 people per km^2 Area 438km^2
Traffic and congestion	◆ Car ownership high: 5% have three or more cars. 2.5 million cars but 35% have no cars. ◆ Congestion charge since 2003 has reduced traffic by 20%. Extended in 2007.	◆ Car ownership low: 90% use public transport; great mix of traffic types ◆ Seven islands so lots of bottlenecks ◆ 590 vehicles per km ◆ 6000 road deaths a year
Waste disposal	◆ 4m tonnes a year ◆ Recycling of paper, glass, plastic and metals ◆ Export waste to 18 landfill sites or abroad	◆ 5000 tonnes of solid waste a day ◆ A lot dumped by roads or in rivers
Pollution	◆ Clean Air Acts have reduced air pollution ◆ Less industry ◆ Chief cause is cars = photochemicals	◆ Garbage burning ◆ Use of biofuels in homes ◆ Heavy industry ◆ Two stroke vehicle engines
Water supply	◆ Reservoirs, e.g. Lee Valley, water transfers, Thames and wells ◆ Groundwater table is sinking ◆ Frequent leaks as old pipes	◆ Rely on lakes ◆ Demand exceeds supply ◆ Unreliable in dry season ◆ Shanty areas rely on rain as no piped water ◆ Often polluted
Sanitation	◆ Piped sewage ◆ Dumped offshore or dried and recycled as fertiliser	◆ Rare in shanty areas ◆ Pollutes rivers, etc ◆ Latrines leach into groundwater
Dereliction	◆ Redundant docklands and industrial sites ◆ Toxic contamination ◆ Regeneration schemes, e.g. Canary Wharf, 2012 Olympics sites	◆ Redundant docklands ◆ Old cotton mills ◆ Squatter occupied ◆ Little funds for redevelopment

Quick check questions

1 Why has car ownership increased so rapidly in LEDC urban areas?

2 Why are a) landfill and b) incineration not the ideal answers to urban waste disposal?

3 How is 'photochemical smog' produced in urban areas?

4 What has been the main cause of urban sprawl?

5 Why does building on floodplains increase the risk of flooding in urban areas?

How can urban areas be managed sustainably?

Student book pages 203–09

Management challenges

Management challenges entail how to balance the environmental needs (e.g. hydrology and vegetation) against economic needs (e.g. employment and transport) and social needs (e.g. decent housing, cultural, entertainment and historic/cultural aspects).

Sustainability is the ability to carry the system on into the future without a reduction in the system or standard of living.

Key words

Ecological footprint	Social housing
Carbon neutral	Key workers
NIMBY = not in my back yard	

Exam tips

You may wish to question the whole notion of sustainability. If you do, then keep this to the conclusion of an extended answer.

Sustainability is about reducing inputs (e.g. energy, water and raw materials) and reducing harmful outputs (e.g. pollution) but also about ensuring flows in the system are efficient (e.g. transport)

Issues for managing urban areas:

- What is the exact nature of the environmental and water resources and their status (quality versus quantity)?
- Sheer cost – short versus long term, e.g. the damage traffic does to the urban roads. Who should pay? Local versus national issue – rate payer (or driver or owner) versus tax payer.
- Who pays versus who gains? Should tax payers subsidise developments that benefit a small group, e.g. drivers? The construction of eco-towns exemplifies this and the Nimbyism this produces. How effective is the scheme and for whom?
- Political will, e.g. London is in reality much bigger in area and population than the Greater London Council and covers parts of a large number of other authorities such as Essex and Surrey.

- Technology – has the area the knowledge and expertise to develop the challenging urban environment? Is enough known about that particular environment?
- Size or scale – definition of the area that makes up the project area; it is easier to manage smaller areas such as a local neighbourhood compared to a city.
- How long will it take – quick fix versus long term? Urban areas are dynamic so developments can't be too long term in realisation, e.g. Thames Gateway.
- Wider impacts. What implications are there for areas beyond the project area, e.g. London's ecological footprint is 125 times as large as the city.
- Can cities ever be sustainable? If not, where can all those people go? Is it better to concentrate or spread the problems? Concentrations may be easier to deal with.

Approaches to sustainability

- Regulation, e.g. Clean Air Act, green belts
- Planning and design, e.g. integrated transport, building design
- Economic, e.g. landfill taxes, congestion charging
- Technology, e.g. solar panels, electric vehicles
- Admit defeat, e.g. encourage urban depopulation.

Key words

Eco-town	Reclamation
Recyling	

Exam tips

You need to be able to contrast attempts at urban sustainability. These case studies are contrasted in terms of scale but it could be MEDC versus LEDC.

Case studies: different scales

Very local – Bedzed

The Beddington Zero Energy Development was completed in 2002 in the London Borough of Sutton:

◆ Built on reclaimed land

◆ 82 homes (10 for key workers and 15 affordable homes for social housing)

◆ Houses face south for heat and offices north for shade

◆ Designed to be fully insulated so heated by occupants and appliances, e.g. cookers and solar panels

◆ Built from natural, recycled or reclaimed materials

◆ Zero use of fossil fuel – combined heat and power plant using waste

◆ Layout designed to favour pedestrians and cyclists.

Urban district – Stockholm

The Hammarby scheme in southern Stockholm aims at sustainability by:

◆ energy – residents will produce more than 50 per cent of their energy needs from combustible waste which is burned for power production. Energy is also generated from solar panels and cells

◆ waste – block-based recycling using underground waste disposal pipes for sorted waste. Organic waste is converted into fertiliser while paper, glass and metal are recycled

◆ sewage – used to produce biogas and heat from the treated water is used for district heating and to power buses and vans

◆ transport – the target is for 80 per cent of journeys to be on public transport or bicycle. There is a carpool system and a network of cycle paths.

Town – Eco-towns in the UK

> Student book page 207

In July 2007 the UK government asked for bids to build new towns of 5000–20,000 people that were to:

◆ be carbon neutral in construction and operation

◆ have 50 per cent affordable housing

◆ have lots of open spaces and gardens

◆ have shops and services within walking distance

◆ have houses built from timber

◆ be highly insulated and with solar panels.

Currently there are ten sites designated.

City – Shanghai

> Student book pages 208–09

Dongtan, a new city built on an island in the Yangtze, aims at sustainability by:

◆ energy – entirely from renewable sources: wind farms, solar and biogas

◆ water supply – use of grey water: recycled drainage water to supply toilets, irrigation, etc

◆ food supply – will produce all its own milk, eggs and vegetables. Hydroponics will produce rice

◆ transport – use of hydrogen-fuelled buses. Streets laid out to favour public transport, bikes and pedestrians

◆ environment – mixture of high-density housing, parks, forests, golf course and a wetland park.

Wider planning

Following the Rio de Janeiro Earth Summit in 1992, governments decided that each local authority had to draw up its own strategy for sustainable development. In the UK this initiative was referred to as Local Agenda 21. Sustainable development and the involvement of the local community in the planning of any development is at the core of every strategy. Agenda 21 listed a number of key areas for urban sustainability:

◆ Promoting sustainable land-use planning and management (use of brownfield sites, etc)

◆ Promoting the integrated provision of environmental infrastructure – water, sanitation, drainage and solid-waste management (promoting recycling)

◆ Promoting sustainable energy (reducing the reliance on fossil fuels) and transport systems (away from private cars) in human settlements

◆ Promoting sustainable construction industry activities – using carbon neutral materials.

Increasingly, however, there is opposition to new developments. They may be sustainable in a day-to-day sense and may even be built from recycled or renewable materials, but they still occupy land that once grew crops or sheltered an ecosystem.

Eco-towns have been stalled in the UK by protests and only two of the proposed ten are currently (2009) likely to be built. The disruption caused by construction of these towns (noise, lorries, etc) and the impact the additional new buildings could have on local flooding are two of the main objections.

So even if urban areas themselves can be made self-sustaining, it is unlikely that they will be sustainable in the broader sense.

Quick check questions

1 What do the initials 'NIMBY' stand for?

2 What is the size of London's ecological footprint?

3 In Hammarby, how is the sewage used to increase urban sustainability?

4 What is an 'eco-town'?

5 Why might locating Dongtan where it is be a possible problem in the future?

ExamCafé

Sample questions

 (a) *Briefly describe the pattern of urban land use shown in Figure 1 (n.b. figure not included).* [4 marks]

Student Answer

In the centre there is the CBD with its shops and offices. Around it is a zone of terraced housing. Beyond are semi-detached houses with some parks and industrial sites. At the edge are detached houses built as estates with some industrial estates.

This is a weak answer as it doesn't suggest a pattern nor does it relate sufficiently to the figure. This would not get out of the lower level – probably 2. As a contrast:

Student Answer

The overall pattern is roughly concentric zones with a sector of industry along the railway to the south-east. These concentric zones expand in size from the inner zone outwards.

This is already a more effective answer as it refers to patterns and refers to the figure, and so is likely to be seen as a higher level response.

(b) *Suggest two ways political factors can influence the pattern of urban land use.* [6 marks]

◆ Candidates could take this several ways depending on their view of the scale of this. So, different political systems can have major contrasts in land use such as the rigidly planned cities of the communist era whilst on a smaller scale there are the local authority planning controls and land-use zoning. Others could look at types of controls such as taxation, rent controls, subsidies, publicly owned land uses, e.g. schools.

Remember: if you do more than two factors, only the best two will be marked. Don't try to be clever and do three or more. You will be wasting time and marks.

(c) *Outline two factors that influence the level of traffic congestion in urban areas.* [6 marks]

◆ Here it is always good to give very different factors. Clearly the volume of traffic is crucial but that needs developing perhaps in terms of high car ownership/usage or why it's so high such as during 'rush hour'. Another aspect could be the road capacity such as its size, pattern or number of junctions.

(d) *For one or more named areas, explain the strategies used to reduce the level of urban pollution.* [9 marks]

◆ This is a big question as it involves a range of types of pollution. So, how do you cover forms of urban pollution such as air, water, solids, thermal, light, noise or visual? One way is to pick two major causes of a variety of forms of pollution and look at how these are being tackled. Clearly traffic is a major cause of a lot of these types of pollution so that's one where a range of strategies have been tried. Another might be industry. An alternative approach is to look at a range of the type of strategies such as regulation, laws and planning.

◆ As always with these types of questions, it is best to look at one area in depth or a contrasting pair rather than looking at a great variety with the 'e.g. Mumbai' type approach to exemplifying. Depth and detail are important in lifting you to the higher levels.

Essay questions

With reference to located examples, examine the problems of managing the growing demand for services in urban areas. [25 marks]

◆ This essay is not just about the rising demand for private and public services in urban areas; it is about managing it. This implies that the supply side needs to be looked at as well. This would be a good opportunity to compare an urban area in a MEDC with a LEDC one as clearly the level of resources available would be very different.

◆ As in all essays, the conclusion is crucial. At AS level you are not expected to evaluate but an effective conclusion might go some of the way:

Student Answer

The essential problem is a mismatch between demand and supply – too much demand and too little supply (1) – but in reality it is more complex than that. Demand is dynamic and varies between sections of the community (2) and between locations within the urban area (3). Who decides on the relative priority of these demands and what criteria are used (4)? Should limited resources be concentrated to meet the most extreme demand or be spread to keep more people happy (5)? Who will pay for all this and how (6) – via taxation, local taxes, charges or what? Essentially the problem is about rationing limited resources but what is the most effective and/or fair way of doing that? (7)

(1) the basic idea is repeated (links back to both the question and, one hopes, the introduction)

(2) shows understanding that demand is not fixed but changes with time and between subgroups in the community

(3) good to see some appreciation of geography – i.e. things vary between locations (good to contrast MEDC and LEDC urban areas here) and possibly with scale

(4) one of the key problems – who is to decide and how – various different political systems have different criteria, e.g. communist versus totalitarian versus democracy

(5) again, one of the classic dilemmas. Spread may reduce political opposition but often it is spread too thin to be effective and self-sustaining. Hopefully it acts as seed corn for greater self-help!

(6) again a major issue. To what extent should the end user contribute to the cost of the service? Do we value and cherish that which we get free? Could efficiency be increased by charging?

(7) the essential battle between what is efficient/effective and what is fair – the latter is a point worth discussing as 'fair' may mean different things to different people at different times.

◆ Clearly this is a high-level conclusion but it is a bit lacking in geography – a sense of place. Hopefully this was provided by the preceding paragraphs. This also illustrates how important it is to make sure you have left yourself enough time to do a full and effective conclusion.

Chapter 6
Managing rural change

Student book pages 214–49

Characteristics of rural areas

Student book pages 216–25

Rural areas are areas where:

◆ the bulk of the land is not built on, being farmland or moorland, etc

◆ the major industry and employer is agriculture and/or forestry

◆ there is a low population density with few urban centres

◆ there is a distinctive non-urban culture and lifestyle.

Functions

Functions of rural areas include: residential, services, agricultural, quarrying, forestry, industrial, tourism, military training, nature reserves, water supply and recreational.

Rural land-use patterns

Patterns could be the type of land use or its shape – concentric, linear or amorphous.

> **Exam tips**
>
> Various models have been suggested to explain rural land-use patterns. Rather dated but still with some relevant logic is that of Von Thunen.

Patterns of farming and rural land use may reflect the following factors:

Physical factors:

◆ Climate – highland areas = sheep; warm/sunny areas = fruit and vines

◆ Relief – flat land = arable; steep slopes = sheep, aspect

◆ Drainage – wet areas = cattle, rice; dry areas = sheep; lakes = reservoirs

◆ Soils – fertile soils = arable; infertile = moorland/forest; alkali soils = cereals

◆ Geology – hard rocks = quarries.

Economic factors:

> **Key words**
>
> | | |
> |---|---|
> | Intensive | Subsistence |
> | Extensive | Agri-business |

◆ Distance – farming less intensive (more pastoral) with distance from town as inputs more expensive with distance

◆ Capital – lack of capital = pastoral

◆ Transport – good transport = cash crops (e.g. market gardening)

◆ Labour supply – lack of labour = pastoral; plenty of labour = market gardening

◆ Demand from consumers, industry etc – many crops have bi-products, e.g. cotton = lint and oil.

Social factors:

◆ Population type – e.g. nomads keep animals, not static crops

◆ Religion – some religions favour certain activities

◆ Culture – e.g. Fulani (northern Nigeria) measure their status and wealth in cattle

◆ Education – the more educated tend to be more progressive.

Historical factors:

◆ Inertia – not easy to change farming type as large investment in equipment, etc

◆ Where change is common, pastoral farming is common as investment is mobile

Political factors:

◆ Planning = land use zoning, National Parks, etc

◆ Land ownership, farm size (inheritance laws)

◆ Government policies – quotas, subsidies, etc, e.g. EUCAP, set-aside, etc.

Case study: two contrasting farming areas

	East Anglia – cereals, sugar beet and rapeseed	Southern Nigeria – tree crops, e.g. oil palm, cocoa, rubber
Physical	Warm sunny summers Cold winters with frosts Dry Flat land for machinery Glacial fertile soils Well drained as underlying chalk	Hot humid climate all year High all year rainfall Fertile river silts
Economic	Large scale agri-businesses Reduces costs by growing crops that can be machine harvested Bulk transport Needs little labour Large scale farms Demand from London and agri-industries = brewing, sugar, oils	Plantations owned by TNCs Run like factories so need constant output Near coast for ports Plenty of cheap labour Large scale farms Demand from exporting and local industries = rubber, soap, oils
Social	Well educated Declining farming population	Poorly educated High birth rate so growing farming population
Historical	Long history of arable but was once sheep area for wool trade, e.g. Worsted	Long history from colonial times – British used area as source of raw materials
Political	Influenced by CAP Reduction in subsidies has forced cut in costs = more mechanisation	Influenced by Government's need for exports to pay for development

Settlement patterns

Student book pages 216–17

There are three aspects to settlement pattern:

◆ Horizontal – spacing of settlements; even, regular, random

◆ Vertical – the settlement hierarchy and its functions

◆ Individual settlement shape – linear, nucleated, dispersed, etc.

Causes of settlement patterns

Many are historical. In England, most rural settlements are recorded in the Domesday Book of 1086. Once established, inertia kept them in existence although some vanished due to the Black Death (1348–50) wiping out the whole village.

◆ Physical factors – these dominate as settlements grow up, usually based on farming, e.g. fertile soils, water supply, shelter, timber and building material supply. They are often shown in place names, e.g. 'ley' means a clearing in a wood.

◆ Economic factors – these tend to control which villages expand into towns, e.g. transport routes, power (wind or water mills)

◆ Social factors – often villages set up 'daughter settlements', e.g. Great and Little Tew near Oxford. Some grew up around abbeys or large houses supplying their needs.

Key words

Range	High order goods
Threshold	Low order goods

Exam tips

This topic is most likely to come up via a short question using a map, possibly an OS map, to identify patterns of settlement.

Factors that influence the opportunities and development of rural areas

Student book pages 217–25

Why do some areas develop more rapidly than others?

> **Exam tips**
>
> An initial advantage is often then sufficient to give an area the ability to develop more rapidly via cumulative causation and the multiplier effect.

- ◆ Physical conditions: climate, relief, drainage, soil type, vegetation, water supply, rock type.
- ◆ Economic factors:
  - – Transport – density and type of routes
  - – Accessibility to large urban area
  - – Ability to outbid for sites
  - – Size of site available
  - – Mutual attraction/repulsion – e.g. pig farms and residential
  - – Availability of raw materials – e.g. sand and gravel, crops
  - – Nature of local and regional demand for rural produce
  - – Availability of labour – quantity, quality, price
  - – Existing rural industries – e.g. sugar refining.
- ◆ Social factors:
  - – Historical – conservation, e.g. National Park, reputation, tradition, culture
  - – Mutual attraction/repulsion
  - – Population size, type and characteristics
  - – Land ownership – estate development, e.g. National Trust
  - – Religious factors
  - – Inertia – difficult to change activities, e.g. forestry.
- ◆ Political factors:
  - – Planning controls – National parks, SSSIs, nature reserves
  - – Controls on farming, e.g. CAP, set-aside
  - – Development schemes, e.g. release of green belt
  - – Government uses, e.g. military ranges.

Case study: two rural areas

Student book pages 218–25

	West Oxfordshire	Eastern Cape, South Africa
Environment	30% of area is Cotswold AONB Much is grassland for sheep and pockets of woodlands	Hostile with low variable rainfall so much is uncultivated scrubland
Historical	Land ownership has been crucial – large estates such as Duke of Marlborough's	Afrikaans area which was resettled as 'homelands' in 1970s under apartheid
Farming	Increase in high yielding cereals but sheep in remoter high areas Declined as a source of employment	Largely poor-quality pastoral Subsistence with some arable near rivers – vegetables and maize Yields low
Industry	Traditional rural industries of wool, e.g. Witney, furniture, quarrying	None
Settlement	Villages with market towns such as Chipping Norton	Townships of resettled people. No real hierarchy
Infrastructure	Two main roads A40 and A44 Railway line to Oxford	Little water (e.g. 3km walk to get it), power or sanitation Few local services Two main roads but few local tracks
Social	Ageing population with high percentage of retired people Low birth rate Relatively prosperous population	Most men migrate away for work so unbalanced gender ratio Poverty and unemployment widespread Youthful population so high birth rate
Opportunities	Increase in hi-tech and science parks, e.g. Begbroke Increase in tourism, e.g. Blenheim Increase in second homes and commuter homes, e.g. Charlbury	Increase in tourism Many commute to work in coastal cities

Rural change – causes/ issues

Student book pages 226–37

Key words

Counterurbanisation   Infrastructure

Suburbanisation   Inertia

Causes of change include:

◆   Population change – migration, birth rate, ethnic mix, age structure

◆   Social change – decreased household size, more single person households

◆   Mobility change – increased car ownership and declining public transport

◆   Incomes and wealth – increased or decreased, crop/livestock prices change

◆   Attitudes – desire for and satisfaction with urban or rural lifestyles

◆   Political – planning initiatives, creating conservation areas, land use zoning

◆   Employment structure/location – agricultural versus services

◆   Changing technology – rise of Internet so can work from home, mechanisation of agriculture

◆   Increased leisure time – growth of tourism and recreation

◆   Perception of danger, security, crime risk, etc

◆   Changing infra-structure – gas, water, electricity, TV, etc

◆   Public services – growth or decline type, location.

Issues that result from change

Physical issues:

◆   Relief – building on unsuitable sites, e.g. steep slope

◆   Drainage – water shortage, pollution

◆   Vegetation – loss of habitats

◆   Pollution – air, water, land, noise, visual.

Economic issues:

◆   Power – shortage, reliability, high cost

◆   Industry – lack of jobs or low pay, migrant labour

◆   Settlement – housing quality and quantity, cost, second homes

◆   Services – lack of sufficient schools, shops, clinics, etc

◆   Transport – cost, poor public transport.

Social issues:

◆   Wealth inequality and deprivation

◆   Cultural change

◆   Age profile – dependency ratio, birth rates, social services

◆   Migration – depopulation.

Student book pages 230–37

	Oxfordshire – growth	Eastern Cape – decline
Factors causing change	Expansion of Oxford beyond its green belt Attractive scenery Good link to London via train or M40	Impoverished population isolated on remote former homeland area – overcrowded and high natural increase Increased freedom to move
Developments	Increased housing, e.g. Blackbird Leys Increased recreation, e.g. college sports grounds, golf courses, football stadium New business parks, e.g. nano-technology at Begbroke Park and ride schemes (five) Increased arable farming	Road improvement – more all-weather roads and bridges means more could migrate for work Subsistence farming replaced by cash so less labour needed
Environmental impacts	Loss of habitats Increased flood risk Increased pollution – chiefly from traffic and modern farming, e.g. eutrophication	Loss of wildlife (used for food) Soil erosion from clearing the bush for fuel, etc Water pollution
Economic impacts	Increased road congestion as more traffic Soaring house prices Decline in primary jobs Increase in service jobs – often skilled and well paid Loss of rural services as many commute, e.g. post offices Growth of mini-industrial areas, e.g. Chipping Norton	Rising unemployment Rising poverty Very poor road maintenance Lack of skills (only 4%) Most work as migrant labourers Agriculture in decline (30% uncultivated) Farms and houses left derelict
Social impacts	Friction between 'locals' and wealthy newcomers Increased social activities, e.g. music groups Closure of rural services, e.g. primary schools as few young children Ageing population	High incidence of HIV and AIDS High percentage of women and elderly as young men migrated for work Traditional culture in decline Youthful population – high birth rate
Political impacts	Traditional rural values under threat	Traditional rural values under threat

Quick check questions

1 Why are rural populations decreasing in LEDCs?

2 What is the main impact of second home ownership in rural areas in the UK?

3 Suggest why rural populations are ageing in most MEDCs.

4 Why are primary schools closing in rural areas in the UK?

5 In the Eastern Cape, what is the main reason why rural populations are declining?

Environmental issues

Student book pages 238–43

Environmental issues in rural areas include:

◆ pollution – air, water (eutrophication), noise, visual, solids

◆ water – scarcity (transfer schemes, use of aquifers, reservoir building)

◆ traffic – congestion, pollution, land use (roads, car parks, garages, etc)

◆ habitat destruction – direct and indirect, species diversity

◆ disease introduction – accidental (e.g. foot and mouth) or planned (myxomatosis)

◆ new species introduced – accidentally or planned

◆ dereliction – visual pollution, safety, health.

Traffic congestion and pollution

Causes:

◆ Increased car ownership and usage
◆ Improved main roads/motorways but these feed into minor narrow rural roads
◆ Increased commuting – daily and at weekends (second homes, etc)
◆ Increased recreation in rural areas
◆ Bottlenecks, e.g. bridges
◆ Slow farm traffic and/or herds/flocks
◆ Decline in public transport.

Problems caused:

◆ Time lost in delays
◆ Increased pollution as slow traffic increases pollution
◆ Accidents – animals killed, etc
◆ High fuel costs as slow and winding roads
◆ Decline in public transport – slowed by congestion, etc.

Management:

◆ National Parks are traffic planning authority
◆ Use of charging policies
◆ Subsidised public transport.

Increasing use for recreation and leisure

Causes:

◆ Increased car ownership
◆ Increased leisure time – shorter working week
◆ Higher real incomes
◆ Diversification from farming, e.g. karting, fishing
◆ Creation of National Parks, etc
◆ Second home ownership.

Problems:

◆ Conflicts with farmers, e.g. trampling crops, fires
◆ Honeypot sites get overused, congested
◆ Increased noise (e.g. karting) and pollution (e.g. litter)
◆ Forces up local prices, e.g. house prices
◆ Second home problems
◆ Road and parking congestion in holiday season.

Management:

◆ Honeypot sites
◆ National Parks, ANOBs, etc
◆ Private ownership – Forestry Commission, National Trust, etc.

Key words

Honeypot	SSSI
ANOB	NNR

Building development

Causes:

◆ Urban sprawl, overspill and counterurbanisation
◆ Family break-up – need for more single person dwellings
◆ Ageing housing stock – much is old and decaying as wooden, etc
◆ Higher rural birth rate
◆ Demand for commuter or second homes.

Problems:

◆ Loss of habitats
◆ Increased risk of flooding – more impervious surfaces
◆ Rise in land prices
◆ Overstretched rural services
◆ New buildings do not fit into traditional village style
◆ Pressure on local infrastructure, e.g. water, power.

Management:

◆ Establishment of key settlements or rural hubs – concentrate development and facilities
◆ Tight planning controls over number, type and style of housing
◆ Use of brownfield sites, e.g. disused quarries, old aerodromes
◆ Development of eco-towns.

Key words

Greenfield site   Eco-town
Brownfield site

Impact of changes in farming

Causes:

◆ Need to reduce costs and increase outputs
◆ Growth of agri-businesses 'mining the soil'
◆ Labour shortages = increased mechanisation
◆ CAP – reduction in subsidies
◆ Increased use of chemicals – pesticides, fertilisers, etc
◆ Cheap foreign produce, e.g. enlargement of EU = competition
◆ Diversification in consumer tastes – quality and variety wanted
◆ Changing technology e.g. increased mechanisation, hydroponics etc.

Problems:

◆ Water pollution – eutrophication
◆ Poisoning or disturbance of wildlife – food chain damaged
◆ Soil erosion
◆ Concentration on a few crops – disease/pest risk
◆ Loss of hedgerows, copses and habitats
◆ Excessive irrigation leading to leaching or waterlogging
◆ Soil compressed by machinery = rapid runoff = floods.

Exam tips

It is important to appreciate that much of the LEDC depends on subsistence food crops yet modern global pressures favour commercial cash crops often for export.

Management:

◆ Set-aside
◆ Organic farming
◆ Hybrid crops (GM crops, Green Revolution)
◆ Deintensification
◆ Nitrate Sensitive Areas
◆ Environmentally Sensitive Areas

Case studies: impacts of modern farming

	East Anglia (MEDC)	India (NIC)
Mechanisation	Led to reduction in hedges, increase in field size and loss of ecosystems Compresses soil structure High cost – fuel pollution	Led to loss of rural jobs = increased rural poverty High cost of fuel, parts, etc
Agri-chemicals	Nitrate pollution = eutrophication Pesticides get into food chain = loss of wildlife Herbicides kill rare plants	Nitrate pollution = eutrophication High cost of chemicals so discriminates against poor Damage to wildlife as little regulation, e.g. DDT
Tenure	Individual farmers bought out by agri-businesses so loss of community	Rich farmers expanded at expense of poor = loss of food subsistence crops = increased rural hunger
Irrigation	Increases crop yields and offsets dry spells but lowers rivers and water table Led to construction of reservoirs	Increases crop yields and offsets dry spells but lowers rivers and water table Excessive irrigation has caused salinisation and droughts
Drainage	Loss of wetland areas Chemicals drain into rivers	Loss of wetland and pollution of drinking water
Limited range of crops	Soil erosion as soil exhausted Danger of pests and disease	Soil erosion and loss of many staple food crops = increased dietary problems Pests/diseases common
Hybrid crops	Tests of GM crops face opposition	60% of crops are hybrids with higher yields: three crops a year but they are more expensive
Impact	Increased output so much that CAP reformed to reduce surpluses	Did turn India into a food exporter by 2000 but now an importer

Land degradation and dereliction

Causes:

- Loss of population – fewer people to maintain area
- Ageing population – too poor or old to renovate property
- Decline in farming or swap to a different form = spare buildings
- Excessive use of soil by agri-businesses
- Local authorities lack funds as low tax base

Problems:

- Decaying property, outbuildings, etc – eyesore and dangerous
- Soil erosion – silting of rivers, dust storms, etc
- Abandoned machinery, overgrown fields, etc.

Management:

- Planning controls
- Taxation of derelict buildings
- Soil conservation
- Organic farming, set-aside, etc.

Exam tips

Remember that rural dereliction often stems from rapid out migration and a decline in farming but it may be only temporary as second home owners often jump at the opportunity to convert old barns.

Case study: environmental issues in Oxfordshire

Student book pages 238–43

	Issues	Possible solutions
Traffic congestion	Increasing due to little road development – at capacity Loss of land for parking High cost of road improvements, e.g. £100m for A40	Double track the railway line from Oxford to Worcester, revive Oxford to Witney line. Improve bus services using guided transit express system
Recreation	Country park at Shotover Day visits to honeypot sites such as Blenheim Golf course construction	Extension of green belt controls Careful management of honeypot sites
Pollution	Increased air pollution Water pollution from roads and farming Plan for new reservoir to store Thames water – construction will cause problems	Close monitoring of pollution levels by water authority – fines for polluters
Farm changes	Increased arable has reduced hedges and increased soil erosion	Set-aside and organic farming to meet needs of Oxford
Dereliction	Rare – as buildings snapped up for second homes	Planning controls
Other	Destruction of green belt – 4000 homes planned to the south Increase in impermeable surfaces = increased flooding Decreased biodiversity	Development confined to old disused rural sites, e.g. Shipton Quarry (5000 homes) Increased flood protection schemes, e.g. Witney Creation of SSSIs and nature reserves

Quick check questions

1 What is 'eutrophication'?

2 Why is traffic such a problem in MEDC rural areas?

3 What do the initials CAP stand for?

4 Why can irrigation result in declining crop yields?

5 In what ways is organic farming more risky than non-organic?

How can rural areas be managed sustainably?

Student book pages 243–49

Management challenges

Management challenges involve how to balance the environmental needs (e.g. wildlife, hydrology and vegetation) against economic factors (e.g. farming, employment and transport) and social factors (e.g. rural way of life and historic/cultural aspects).

Key words

Key settlement	Common Agricultural Policy
Conservation	Core versus periphery

Sustainability is the ability to carry the system on into the future without a reduction in the system or standard of living. It is about reducing inputs (e.g. energy, water, chemicals) and reducing harmful outputs (e.g. pollution, soil erosion) but also about ensuring flows in the system are efficient (e.g. transport).

Exam tips

Remember that areas near to an urban area (or core) will have different issues (in type, scale and solution) than remoter, more peripheral rural areas.

Exam tips

Remember that any development should be looked at in terms of costs/benefits – and to whom these apply.

Issues

◆ What is the exact nature of the environmental and water resources and their status (quality versus quantity)?

◆ Sheer cost – short versus long term. Who should pay? Local versus national issue – rate payer versus user versus tax payer.

◆ Who pays versus who gains. Should tax payers subsidise developments that benefit a small group, e.g. farmers or commuters? For the locals or the newcomers? How effective is the scheme and for whom?

◆ Political will, e.g. Oxford green belt is occupied by at least six local authorities. Ownership – who is responsible for rivers flowing through rural areas?

◆ Technology – has the area the knowledge and expertise to develop the rural environment? Is enough known about that particular environment?

◆ Size or scale – definition of the area that makes up the project area. It is easier to manage smaller ones, e.g. local copse versus New Forest.

◆ How long will it take? Quick fix versus long term, e.g. soil erosion is increasing partly as a result of global warming.

◆ Balancing priorities – economic versus environmental. How do you value scenery?

◆ Wider impacts. What implications are there for areas beyond the project area, e.g. planned new reservoir near Oxford?

Case study: the ways farms adapt to change to try to be more sustainable

	Details	Examples
Specialise	Reduce the range of activities so reducing costs. Specialise in a small range of outputs usually high value, low weight. Very risky if demand or weather change.	Howbarrow Farm in Cumbria is an organic farm growing vegetables, herbs and fruit. In 2001 it started a home delivery service. Also has a farm trail and bed and breakfast.
Diversify – existing activities	Use the existing activities or infrastructure in a different way to diversify the sources of farm income. Not a change in use so unlikely to need planning permission	Hicks Farm in Essex has a farm shop, rents out disused barns for storage and uses its reservoirs for fishing. It is the latter that earns the largest 'profit'.
Diversify into new activities	Develop new activities on the farm that bring in new sources of income so spreading the risk if crop prices fall, etc. Will need planning permission and new build.	Leaches Farm in Buckinghamshire has set up its own business centre of eight office units with a £5000 p.a. rent. It benefits from its proximity to the M40.
Change type of activity	Move out of farming into a new activity often based on tourism or recreation. Limited market and often seasonal.	Old Macdonald's Farm in Essex near the M25 has 50 indoor and outdoor amusements.

Making rural areas more sustainable

Ways of managing and protecting rural areas vary in scale. It is not easy to make rural areas sustainable as there is often a conflict between economic or social sustainability and physical environment sustainability.

Exam tips

You need to be able to contrast attempts at rural sustainability. These are contrasted in terms of scale but it could be MEDC versus LEDC.

Scale	Example	Comment
Local	**SSSI – Site of Special Scientific Interest** Notification of an SSSI will include a statement of the views of Natural England (NE) or the Countryside Council for Wales (CCW) about the management of the land, as well as a list of operations that may be harmful to the special interest. If the owner or occupier wishes to carry out any of these operations they must first obtain consent from NE/CCW.	These fears on preserving rare species or fragile ecosystems, so sustaining them. Management is by agreement with the landowner but if no agreement can be reached then it can be compulsorily purchased. Often very small scale but in total can cover a large area, e.g. 10% of Wales has been so designated. The Pembrokeshire coastal path has 17 SSSIs. Sometimes too small to manage and 'police' effectively
Area	**National Park, Peak District: UK's first in 1951** The Authority acts as a planning authority to control developments seen as harmful to the environment. It offers specialists' advice on entitlement to grants for any work carried out and there are a number of projects aimed at supporting and funding local organisations that are helping conserve and enhance the environment. As well as offering day-to-day guidance, the Authority is also working with its partners to develop mid- to long-term plans and policies which will protect the National Park's landscape and wildlife and sustain its communities by developing the rural economy.	These are more overtly aimed at substainability, especially balancing economic and environmental sustainability. Unlike National Parks elsewhere (e.g. USA) the Park Authority does not own the land and can only control via planning and the use of targeted grants. It is charged with the task of keeping the rural areas vibrant – management not conservation. There is an inevitable conflict between its conservation activities and the need to grant access to visitors.

Scale	Example	Comment
Regional	**Amathole, South Africa** The district council aims to halve unemployment, eradicate poverty, invest in sustainable infrastructure and develop the economy. It will develop livestock farming, develop farming co-operatives, introduce drought resistant fodder crops. It will also develop essential oils based on local plants (high value, low weight product). Focus on improving education and roads.	Here, the focus is mainly on economic sustainability. Progress is slow as it needs large public and private investments to 'kick-start' development. This may be economically and socially sustainable but any success may endanger the natural environment unless it is closely monitored. The area also suffers from a high birth rate and HIV so these may siphon off investment.
National	**UK** Natural England has powers stemming from the National Parks and Access to the Countryside Act 1949 to designate land as a National Nature Reserve (NNR). Each NNR has its own reserve management plan. E.g. Beinn Eighe, Britain's first National Nature Reserve, features striking mountain scenery and ancient pinewoods overlooking Loch Maree. The reserve is home to typical Highland wildlife, including red deer, golden eagles and the pine marten.	These tend to aim at environmental sustainability, sometimes at the expense of economic sustainability. The Land Reform (Scotland) Act 2003 granted a statutory right of responsible access which puts pressure on such reserves. NNRs in Scotland are either managed by Scottish Natural Heritage (SNH), or are privately owned and managed along with the owner under a Nature Reserve Agreement (NRA). Other NNRs are owned and managed by partner organisations who own the land, such as the Forestry Comission, RSPB and the National Trust. Clearly these may have contrasting priorities.
International	**EU** Limestone pavements were given protection under the European Habitats Directive in 1992, when they were recognised as a priority habitat for designation as Special Areas of Conservation (SAC). Priority habitat types are those seen as at risk of development across Europe. Seven areas of pavement in the UK have been identified as possible Special Areas of Conservation (SACs) under the Directive.	These are more overtly aimed at sustainability, especially balancing economic and environmental sustainability. The EU has tried to bring some kind of consistency to its development policies. Rural areas came under Objective 2 funding – where there is low population density, declining population, high unemployment, etc. During the 1990s the CAP introduced set-aside, and promoted organic farming, grants for environmental projects and subsidies for converting arable land to woodland. It is trying to make rural areas economically viable.
Global	**UN** Biosphere Reserves (BR) are areas of terrestrial and coastal/marine ecosystems which are internationally recognised under UNESCO's Man and the Biosphere (MAB) programme launched in 1971, e.g. Braunton Burrows National Nature Reserve in 1976.	Increasingly, key sites are recognised as needing protection but the UN also encourages development in a sustainable way. Ultimately, national interests could conflict with such designations, e.g. plans for an airport on Maplin Sands in Essex – an area of international importance for bird migration.

Quick check questions

1 Farming has been in decline in MEDCs for some time – why might it increase in importance in the future?

2 What is increasingly the activity that is replacing farming as the source of MEDC rural incomes?

3 What do the initials SSSI stand for?

4 What is the main way that official bodies in the UK such as National Parks control rural land uses?

5 Why is rural conservation increasingly viewed at an international scale?

ExamCafé

Sample questions

1 (a) *Study Figure 2 showing settlement hierarchy in an LEDC (n.b. figure not included).*

    i) *Describe the pattern of settlements shown in Figure 2 [4 marks]*

◆ Always remember that the information comes from the figure and you should quote some values or names from the graph. Here there is a clear focus on pattern. Contrast these two responses:

Student Answer [Low-level response]

There are lots of small centres or hamlets with a few larger villages and two market centres.

Student Answer [High-level response]

There are 22 settlements under 120 population in size, five large villages between 1200 and 1500 people and two market centres over 20,000. There is a clear hierarchy with a strong relationship between the number of settlements and their population size although settlement X is a clear anomaly being rated a large village with 250 population.

    ii) *Suggest two reasons why settlement X on Figure 2 does not fit the pattern described in (i) [6 marks]*

◆ Clearly centre X is out of line with the overall trend/pattern. Always remember that this could be due to some factor affecting the x axis or the y axis – here it means could it be due to it having a lower than expected population (e.g. out migration, drought) or higher than expected status (e.g. route centre, tribal centre, tourist stop)? Always make sure your cause–effect is clear to reach the higher level response; i.e. why does a route centre have a higher status?

(b) *Outline two reasons for increasing levels of traffic congestion in rural areas [6 marks]*

◆ Notice that this question does not clarify MEDC or LEDC so it is more generic, nor does it ask for examples but these would help your answer. Again, try to give two contrasting reasons. For example:

Student Answer

Increasing rural affluence has led to higher car ownership so more cars are on the roads but, at the same time, rural roads have not been increased or widened due to the excessive cost so congestion is bound to increase.

◆ This presents a clear contrast but more details and/or examples would have ensured full marks.

(c) *For one or more named rural areas, explain the impact of changes in farming on the local environment.* *[9 marks]*

◆ If you can do this from one rural area, so much the better, as depth will score higher than repetition or breadth of ideas. There is less credit for listing changes than for spelling out their impacts on the environment (physical, economic, social). Again, a key element is cause and effect. Why did that change (e.g. from pastoral to arable farming north-west of Oxford) cause those impacts?

◆ Changes in farming could be the type of farming but equally it could include the methods used, e.g. increased mechanisation, decrease in profitability. It is the impact of these that is crucial.

◆ It is important to note the 's' on the end of change – there must be at least two changes.

Essay questions

With reference to located examples explain how planning and management practices are enabling rural areas to become increasingly sustainable. [25 marks]

◆ This is a challenging question drawn directly from the wording in the specification. It is important to set out your interpretation of rural sustainability from the start as there is a real danger you will see this as about management per se and so launch off into discussing National Parks.

Student Answer

Sustainability (1) is about ensuring that the system can carry on into the future without a reduction in the system or standard of living of the people living there. In rural areas this is a problem as the system is a complex blend of physical, economic and social aspects (2). By making one aspect sustainable it might be at the expense of one or more of the other aspects (3). It is difficult balancing all of these demands on sustainability, especially as they are so dynamic (4). One way is to manage the inputs, outputs, stores and flows in the rural system (5) to ensure it remains or becomes as sustainable as possible (6). To do this requires an integrated approach (7) at a variety of scales.

◆ This is a high-quality introduction as it avoids many of the potential pitfalls yet sets out a clear context for what follows. In this way the candidate can justify the inclusion of a range of planning and management practices that may not always be clearly linked to sustainability (although that would be preferred).

(1) clear definition of sustainability
(2) good recognition that it is not a simple system but a mix of physical and human subsystems
(3) good appreciation that these aspects impact on each other – change one then all will change to some degree
(4) good recognition that this system is dynamic, with all these aspects ever changing
(5) clear understanding of what a system is (this could be one effective but challenging way to structure the rest of the essay)
(6) clear sense of realism here – it is doubtful if an end goal of sustainability can be achieved and then maintained
(7) clear idea of the need to plan/manage in a joined-up way – clearly this essay was going on to look at some of the types of management at these scales.

◆ This question does not require any evaluation of the effectiveness of these practices – AS level does not require this – but if the candidate were to qualify the relative success of the practices then this would demonstrate a higher level response. Another way is to ensure case studies are tightly relevant and have the depth needed to demonstrate a link to the concept of sustainability.

Chapter 7
The energy issue

Student book pages 254–85

Availability of energy – global patterns

Student book pages 256–67

Types and sources of energy

Types of energy are:

- non-renewable – fossil fuels (oil, gas, coal), nuclear
- semi-renewable – wood, biofuels, nuclear
- renewable – wind, tidal, wave, solar, geothermal, water (water wheel and hydro).

Exam tips

This is a good example of the argument about whether humans develop to the level of their resources (Malthus) or, as pressure mounts, they find or develop new resources (Boserup).

Global pattern

	Oil	Coal	Natural gas	Nuclear	Hydro
Where it is the major source	Relatively common but the Middle East has 50%	Asia Pacific at 50%	Europe and Eurasia at 33%	Rare but Europe at 10%	South and Central America at 28%
Reserves	1, 208,000 million barrels	Over 3 trillion tons	181 trillion m³	Few built since Chernobyl	Limited as best sites used
Chief areas of reserves	61.5% Middle East	27% USA	Mid East 41%, Eurasia 35%	Main reserve of uranium in Asia	Asia
Chief user	USA	China	Russia	France	China, Brazil
Fastest growing demand	Asia – China 7% a year	Asia – China double by 2025	Europe and Asia	India and China	South America
Other		Can be used to produce gas and oil	Increasingly from unconventional sources		

Factors influencing energy supply

Student book page 259

The following factors influence energy supply:

- **Physical:** climate (wind, water, solar), relief (water), water supply (thermal), vegetation type and volume (biofuels), tidal range, geology (fossil fuels, geothermal)

- **Economic:** capital, technology, demand, site size, transport (of fuel and energy), cost of fuels/ operation, competition, agriculture, forestry, waste disposal

- **Social:** safety, pollution (air, water, solid – acid rain), noise

- **Political:** cost, security, anti-pollution agreements, opposition from voters, impact on local economy, quotas on renewables, agreement with neighbours/borders (e.g. international rivers).

Case studies: energy rich and energy poor countries

Student book pages 269–74

	UK – energy rich	Mali – energy poor
Current sources	Gas 42%, oil 32%, coal 18%, nuclear 8%	Firewood
Resources	Oil and gas from North Sea but has fallen 30% since 1990 Coal has declined as best seams used up – now import 60% 9 of the 12 nuclear plants scheduled to close by 2020 Unreliable climate is a problem for renewables	No fossil fuels – relies on imports Some biofuels Relies on animal and human power (e.g. ploughing)
Trends	Demand is slowing due to greater efficiency Increasingly importing energy (75% now) Coal and nuclear will close North Sea oil and gas running out Increasing renewables; especially wind Rising cost of energy	Demand rising rapidly due to population growth and urbanisation Running out of firewood Rising energy import bill means less money for development Rising cost of energy
Future	Government set target of 10% from renewable by 2010, e.g. wind farms and river barrages Likely to develop a new range of nuclear plants Increasing energy efficiency	National Domestic Energy Strategy – focus on renewables; especially solar and biofuels Improving energy efficiency, e.g. stoves

Quick check questions

1 Why is wood considered only semi-renewable as a resource?

2 Where are the world's main known oil reserves?

3 Why was the Chernobyl incident so important for the nuclear industry?

4 Explain why the UK both exports and imports oil.

5 What is the main source of fuel in Mali and why is this a problem?

Relationship between energy use and economic development

Student book pages 268–69

There is a positive correlation between energy use and economic development. As one increases, so does the other, but what is the cause and what is the effect?

If economic development increases (e.g. China) then there will be:

◆ more 'spare' or disposable wealth to spend on energy consuming products

◆ increased demand from industries; especially heavy industry

◆ improved transport – increased demand for diesel, petrol, etc

◆ increased demand from agriculture – mechanisation, chemicals, etc.

If energy production or use increases (e.g. Russia) then there will be:

◆ increased foreign exchange earnings and foreign investment

◆ more employment – direct and indirect

◆ improved transport, etc

◆ higher energy tax earnings to be invested in development schemes, etc

◆ growth of industries supplying energy industry, e.g. construction

The issues associated with a rising demand for energy

Reasons for rising demand

Student book page 275

Exam tips

With rising demand and limited supplies there is a real danger of wars breaking out over access to energy. Many see the Iraq War in that context.

Reasons for rising energy demand include:

- increased standards of living, e.g. electrical appliances, cars
- increased population
- changing lifestyles, e.g. use of computers
- increased mobility, e.g. aviation fuel
- increased communication, e.g. phones
- global warming, e.g. air conditioning
- changing technology, e.g. automated manufacturing, farming
- rapid industrialisation, e.g. China
- relative cost of energy.

Exam tips

You will not be asked directly about global warming as it is an A2 topic but it is an important reason why we need to look at reducing our demand for and use of energy.

Issues arising from increased demand for energy

Economic issues:

- Cost of building new power stations and transmission lines
- Shortage of skilled energy workers
- Rising cost of energy
- Regional inequality based on energy resources
- Export versus import of energy
- Energy is needed to develop.

Social issues:

- Health problems living near power stations and pylons
- Energy poverty – old and poor at risk.

Political issues:

- Energy 'wars'
- Energy colonialism.

Environmental issues:

- Fossil fuel combustion is a major source of acid rain, smog and global warming
- Pollution from oil spills and pipeline leaks
- Increased demand for firewood can cause deforestation and desertification
- Visual pollution
- River problems (silting, flooding, etc) from dams.

Global warming – where longwave radiation from the earth is trapped and re-radiated back by greenhouse gases (carbon dioxide, methane, nitrous oxide and CFCs) – is occurring as energy demand increases.

	Causes of global warming	Effects of global warming
Physical	Melting of permafrost releases methane Loss of trees – less CO_2 removed Sun's energy output varies	Climate change – becomes more extreme, e.g. storms Increased disasters, e.g. drought Pests and diseases spread Ice caps vanish Rise in sea level means erosion and flooding Change in wildlife – extinctions
Economic	Burning forests releases CO_2 Burning fossil fuels in cars and factories Cattle produce methane Paddy fields give off methane CFCs released, e.g. from fridges Power stations – waste gases	Change in agriculture means crops and animals change, famine spreads Tourist destinations alter Transport damaged – rails buckle Fires more common Water shortages (rationing) Some industries expand, e.g. cooling Increased cost of energy
Social	Increased population produces more CO_2 and methane	Heat waves and severe winters increase death rate More exotic diseases and pests More flooding Need for air conditioning

Case studies: energy impacts

Student book pages 275–78

	Norway = benefits	Nigeria = problems
Background	4.5m people. Seventh largest oil producer and third largest exporter	130 million people. Sixth largest oil exporter
Reserves	All oil and gas offshore 850 hydro plants generate 99% of electricity	In delta and offshore, 159 small oil fields Reserves are being exhausted
Environmental	Minimal impact due to strict control, inspections, etc Potential to damage marine ecosystem and fishing industry	Largest mangrove forest destroyed by pollution, land clearance, etc Flaring of gas causes acid rain Tanker movement has increased shore/reef erosion Water and air pollution
Economic	33% of export earnings 80,000 directly employed 250,000 in indirect oil jobs Boosted technological development Attracted heavy power using industries – e.g. electro chemicals Has renewable energy programme	90% of export earnings Many jobs go to foreigners as skilled Dominated by five TNCs, e.g. Shell No longer self-sufficient in food as focused on oil Imports the bulk of its fuel as refineries old/inefficient Increased import of luxury goods
Social	Oil revenue used to boost welfare system High standard of living High spending in rural areas has reduced rural depopulation	Little trickling down of wealth Over 20 ethnic groups in area – fight over lack of oil wealth
Political	Invested oil revenue abroad – $150 billion Ownership of the seabed issues	Corruption siphons off up to 70% of oil revenue Nationalised oil industry in 1971 Little preparation for future Rebel groups attack pipelines and kidnap workers

Quick check questions

1 Explain why a reduction in burning fossil fuels will have little impact on global warming.

2 Why is Europe so vulnerable to changes in fuel prices?

3 Explain why Norway can export so much of its oil.

4 Why has Nigeria not benefited as it might from its income from oil exports?

5 Why do LEDCs rely on TNCs to develop energy resources?

Managing energy to ensure sustainability

Student book pages 279–85

Management challenges

Management challenges include how to balance the economic needs (e.g. power for industry, jobs, etc) against environmental needs (e.g. reducing pollution, subsidence) and social needs (e.g. energy equality, historic/cultural aspects, etc).

Sustainability is the ability to carry the system on into the future without a reduction in the system or standard of living.

Key words

Ethanol	Retro-fitting
Hybrid engines	Carbon trading
Photovoltaic	

Management involves reducing or conserving inputs (e.g. fuel, water, raw materials) and reducing harmful outputs (e.g. pollution) but is also about ensuring flows in the system are efficient (e.g. transport of energy).

Management issues:

◆ What is the exact nature of the fuel and water resources and their status (quality versus quantity)?

◆ Time – should areas conserve energy resources for the future or should they share them with others? This gives some countries great political influence, e.g. Russia, or triggers wars.

◆ Sheer cost – short versus long term, e.g. damage mining or energy production does to the environment. Who should pay? Local versus national issue – rate payer versus tax payer versus energy user.

◆ Who pays versus who gains? Should tax payers subsidise developments that benefit a small group, e.g. industrialists? The construction of nuclear power stations (e.g. Sizewell in Suffolk) exemplifies this and the NIMBYism this produces. How effective is the scheme and for whom? What are the benefits and to whom?

◆ Political will – do local authorities, TNCs or central government control schemes; e.g. wind farms off the north Wales coast? Much of this debate requires countries to co-operate (e.g. Kyoto agreement – will this overcome political self-interest?).

◆ Technology – has the area the knowledge and expertise to develop the facilities or does it have to attract TNC investment? Is enough known about that particular technology or environment?

◆ How long will it take? Quick fix versus long term. Demand is rapidly rising so developments can't be too long term in realisation, e.g. a single power station is much quicker than a multi-purpose river scheme.

◆ Wider impacts. What implications are there for areas beyond the project area? E.g. British coal-fired power stations used to pollute Scandinavia with acid rain.

◆ Can energy production ever be sustainable without a vast drop in its output? If not, what do we need to change in our economies/cultures?

Exam tips

The MEDCs are trying to conserve and reduce energy consumption but this is in the face of NICs and LEDCs needing to increase energy consumption to meet the expectations of their growing populations.

Sustainability is about balancing supply and demand

Supply:

1 Expand energy production – build new plant, discover new oilfields, etc

2 New technology, e.g. nuclear fusion, recover more oil from oil wells

3 Diversify energy production – new sources (within the area or from other external suppliers) or new fuels

4 Increase renewable, e.g. fast breeder reactor, tidal

5 Reduce loss in transfer – better and more efficient grids

6 Reduce waste, e.g. flaring off gas, use heat produced in the home such as body heat.

Demand:

1 Ration energy – raise price, e.g. petrol tax, have quotas

2 Reduce consumption, e.g. insulation, long-life light bulbs

3 Make machinery more energy efficient, e.g. long-life bulbs, remove 'standby' mode on equipment

4 Increase public's awareness of energy use, e.g. education, media.

How can we conserve energy?

Governments can:

◆ set a high level of tax on petrol, fuel oil, etc

◆ set legal limits on fuel consumption requirements for cars, etc

◆ subsidise home insulation or energy generation, e.g. solar panels

◆ encourage recycling (fines, monitor bins, incentives, etc)

◆ set laws to set minimum energy efficiency standards

◆ monitor the use of energy in buildings, etc.

Individuals can:

◆ walk or cycle rather than drive

◆ make more multi-purpose trips

◆ use public transport

◆ use carpooling

◆ use low energy bulbs and equipment

◆ improve house insulation

◆ not leave appliances on standby.

Key words

Insulation	Recycling
Energy efficiency	Heat exchanger

Exam tips

Individuals are encouraged to conserve or reduce energy but they can only have a minor impact. It needs concerted government action to have a significant impact.

Increase renewables

Student book pages 280–84

Renewable energy	Advantages	Disadvantages
Solar power: photovoltaic systems (e.g. Japan), solar power stations (e.g. California)	Can be small scale and meet local needs Easy to install Long life	Needs high percentage of sun days Can corrode in acid rain, etc Low output currently
Wind power (e.g. Germany)	Can be small scale and meet local needs Ever increasing in efficiency	Relatively inefficient Eyesore – often on highland Noise
Biomass: fuelwood, ethanol (e.g. Brazil), biodiesel (e.g. Germany)	Can use agricultural waste Anyone can grow it Low-level technology so cheap to use	Takes over land used for food crops causing famine Can cost more energy to grow and harvest the crop Vulnerable to climate, pests, etc
Geothermal: hot springs (e.g. Iceland, Hawaii)	Very cheap and 100% natural Long life Not controlled by weather	Needs heat source near the surface Often in tectonically active area Salts, etc, can build up and block pipes, etc
Tidal power: barrages across estuaries (e.g. France)	Not controlled by weather Minimal running costs once built Multi-purpose schemes	Needs a large tidal range May damage estuarine ecosystem Very expensive to build Can cause silting and disrupts wildlife
Wave energy (e.g. Scotland)	Can be small scale and meet local needs	Depends on type and frequency of waves Needs deep water coast Expensive compared to output of energy High maintenance

Case study: Germany

Student book pages 284–85

- Fifth largest energy consumer
- Oil (36%), gas (23%) and coal (24%) but only has coal reserves
- Renewables 5% in 2006
- Hydro 5% – in pre-Alps area
- Renewable Energy Sources Act set minimum price guarantee for 20 years and tax concessions

- Has 52% of world's solar panels – including one site of 62 acres
- In 2007, had over 18,000 wind turbines – flat North German plain and now offshore
- Investing in bioenergy from crops in north Germany
- Sees renewables as an important industrial sector for the future.

Case study: multi-purpose river scheme – Kainji Dam on the Niger in Nigeria

- Built 1964–68 – major symbol of independence
- The dam is one of the longest dams (10kms) in the world – cost £209m
- Produces 800 MW from 10 turbines
- Supplies electricity for all the large Nigerian cities and some is exported to Niger
- Saves using oil which can then be exported
- Created a 135 km long, 30km wide lake, which is used as a reservoir and by the fishing industry
- Water can be used to irrigate crops creating cash/commercial farming
- Created Nigeria's first National Park in 1976 around the lake
- Development of tourism at north-west end of the lake

- New crossing point via dam of Niger
- Ship lock and lake has improved navigation on the seasonal river.

But there are risks of being so dependent on one scheme:

- Lack of maintenance so much of the equipment is now obsolete
- Silting (and high evaporation) is reducing the lake's capacity
- Fishermen have overfished the lake
- Flood in 1998 has shifted the dam slightly so threatening it
- Should the dam burst, millions would die downstream and Nigeria would lose its energy supply.

Exam tips

Multi-purpose river schemes are good examples of 'green energy' and for many LEDCs they offer other gains besides cheap (once built) energy.

Quick check questions

1 Why is the supply of fossil fuels likely to fall?

2 What is the main way used to ration energy supplies?

3 What is the chief problem of wind power?

4 Why is the Severn Estuary in the UK ideal for tidal energy production?

5 In what sense are biofuels a mixed blessing?

Sample questions

(a) *Study Figure 3, a map showing the proven global oil reserves (n.b. figure not included). Briefly describe the pattern of reserves shown. [4 marks]*

◆ Remember that 'pattern' requires something other than a list. Here this is not so easy to define as 62 per cent lies in the Middle East so it is probably best to contrast continents or possibly MEDCs versus LEDCs. Always remember to quote figures and places from the map/diagram as this lifts answers to the higher level.

(b) *Outline two economic factors that influence the level of energy production. [6 marks]*

◆ This is tricky as it is easy to miss 'production' and so focus on consumption. They are rarely the same. Cause and effect need to be clear:

Student Answer

If a country lacks capital to invest in power plants then energy production will be low and it will not have the technology to develop production sites such as dams or wind farms.

◆ A sound attempt but a little superficial and the cause–effect could have been more developed:

Student Answer

Power stations cost a lot to be built – over £20m for an oil-fired station – so if an area lacks sufficient 'spare' capital it will not be built and so production remains low. If there is a large demand in the area for energy it will bid up the price of energy and so encourage new producers to enter the market, so increasing production.

◆ Clearly a higher level answer. It is worth noting that the first answer nowhere near filled up the allocated space. This should have alerted the candidate to adding some more detail such as an example.

(c) *Suggest two reasons why energy consumption increases as a country develops. [6 marks]*

◆ Remember that this is a reflexive relationship. Energy consumption can increase development – it powers industrialisation (it is one of the pre-conditions to take off in the Rostow model) but, more likely, development demands more energy to power the new gadgets, communications, etc.

◆ So your answer could give two contrasting reasons or pick two from the same side of the relationship.

(d) With reference to located examples, examine the development of renewable energy resources. [9 marks]

◆ The term 'located examples' is used to indicate an example of a place is required; not a type of renewable energy. Remember this is a Geography exam and try to use located examples wherever you can.

◆ The term 'development' is open to interpretation – it could mean the actual construction of various renewable energy resources (e.g. an offshore wind farm) or it could mean the development of renewables in general. By using the term 'examine', the examiner has left the interpretation flexible but there is the implication that some explanation or reasoning behind this development is expected.

Essay questions

With reference to located examples, examine the problems created by the exploitation of energy resources for people and the environment. [25 marks]

◆ This is one of those awkward questions for candidates as it has more than one element. There is a clear stress on problems created by exploitation of energy resources (both in terms of extracting from the ground/river, etc, **and** in the generation of energy by power stations) **but** candidates need to focus on both the environment and people. There is no requirement for the two aspects to be given equal coverage but you can't dismiss one aspect in a few sentences.

◆ 'People' is more complex than 'the environment' as people are not identical or uniform:

Student Answer

The exploitation of oil and gas in Alaska (1) has created vast problems for the local indigenous Inuit. It isn't simply the carving up of their traditional hunting lands into oil claims or the impact of drilling that has poisoned much of the ground and rivers in which they fished (2) but it is also the injection of an alien wealthy population into a largely subsistence lifestyle (3). Some Inuit work for the oil companies (4) but many become depressed at the changes and become ill or alcoholics (5). Inequalities of wealth increase in the community (6) driving a wedge into the traditional culture especially between the young and old (7). Crime and vice appear where once they were unknown (8). It doesn't stop there as the oil has to be transported out of this difficult area. Pipelines cross the north slope raised on legs to insulate them from the permafrost but this creates barriers to the caribou which the Inuit hunted and new 'oil roads' encourage more young people to leave the area (9).

(1) clearly located but a pity there are no exact place names
(2) more environmental problems but then linked to the community's economic activity
(3) good point about contrast in populations and good use of geographical vocabulary – 'subsistence'
(4) not all negative – but could have been developed into problems
(5) clear problems but could have been explained more – why are they depressed?
(6) good – a clear people problem for some
(7) well developed to explain where the inequalities are most likely to impact
(8) good point but needs explaining and linking to the oil exploitation
(9) clever to broaden the idea of exploitation to include its transport.

◆ One of the key points about this answer is the overlap with the Cold Environments topic. That really isn't a problem as tourism does much the same. This means you can use the same case study in different contexts. This could reduce your revision.

Chapter 8
The growth of tourism

Student book pages 290–321

Changing patterns of tourism

Student book pages 292–96

Key travel motivators

> **Exam tips**
>
> There is no need in answers to go back a long way in history – 'recent' usually means the last 20 years. Tourism has grown massively since the 1950s.

Prime reasons for travel:
- Leisure – holiday, sport, cultural event, educational, pilgrimage
- Business – conference, meetings, exhibition
- Visiting friends and relations – stay with family, meet friends.

Destination preferences (factors influencing choice of destination):
- Climate – dry, sunny and guaranteed
- Attractions and entertainment
- Festivals and events
- Accommodation
- Facilities, e.g. bars
- Transport to and within destination
- Destination language and culture
- Destination reputation.

Externalities:
- Destination security
- Exchange rate.

> **Key words**
>
> Package tour   Long haul
>
> Globalisation   Disposable income

Changing tourism patterns

- Rapid growth in tourism – over 4 per cent a year
- Europe is still the most important destination but a rapid rise of East Asia and Central America
- Tourism in top five export earners in 83 per cent of countries and number one in 38 per cent
- Rapid growth in tourists from NIC or LEDCs but still dominated by MEDCs
- Rise of specialised types of tourism, e.g. cruises, eco-tourism, religious
- Cheap high volume destinations static or in decline, e.g. southern Spain
- Increase in remoter destinations (long haul), e.g. New Zealand
- Increase in 'second holidays' – especially urban breaks, e.g. Prague
- Increase in multi-centre holidays, e.g. island hopping in Greece.

> **Key words**
>
> Enclave   Niche market
>
> Nomadic tourism   Special interest

> **Exam tips**
>
> The growth of tourism is not just between countries but also within them. The bulk of tourism in MEDCs and China is from their own populations.

Types of tourist destination

	Example	Comment
Tourist enclave	Cancun, Mexico	Separate from local community on its sand bar. Largely self-contained
Resort	Bournemouth, UK	Integrated seaside resort that is diversifying away from beach holidays, e.g. conferences
Holiday village	Center Parcs, Elveden, UK	Purpose-built village with range of facilities and entertainment. Designed for families
City break	Prague, Czech Republic	Became a favourite for stag nights as it is cheap but now trying to move up market and stressing its history and culture
Dark tourism	Somme in France (First World War battlefield)	Increasing in popularity partly due to history but also risks sometimes involved
Sex tourism	Philippines	Visitors from countries that have repressive laws on sexual relations look for more relaxed areas (can lead to criminal acts)
Cultural tourism	Bangkok, Thailand	Trying to attract tourism for the temples, palaces and other cultural attractions
Nomadic tourism	Caribbean cruising	Live on the ship (removed from local culture) but visit a new destination every day

Reasons for growth

Student book pages 292–98

Economic reasons:

◆ Increased leisure time and longer paid holidays

◆ Cheaper and faster types of transport, especially budget airlines

◆ Active marketing by resorts and travel firms

◆ Increased real incomes – more 'spare'

◆ Decreasing real costs of holidays

◆ Globalisation has increased business travel

◆ Rise of the Internet – easier to personalise holidays.

Social reasons:

◆ Increased psychological need to 'escape'

◆ Increased desire to experience different cultures

◆ Rise in lifestyle expectations

◆ Increased education about other areas and their cultures

◆ International migration – more have relatives abroad

◆ Spread of English language

◆ Increased media coverage.

Political reasons:

◆ LEDCs see it as a means to develop – income earner

◆ Government investment in tourism, infrastructure, etc

◆ Removal of restrictions on and barriers to travel.

But – the tourist industry is vulnerable because it is seen as a 'luxury' purchase so demand can fluctuate as the economy does. Individual areas can be hit by disasters, fear of terrorism, health scares, exchange rate fluctuations, etc.

Exam tips

International tourism can be greatly affected by 'external shocks' – economic, political and other factors suddenly reducing demand (e.g. Sars outbreak in China).

Types of tourism

Tourism is classified by:

◆ purpose, e.g. active (e.g. sport) versus passive (e.g. sightseeing)

◆ duration, e.g. day trips versus longer

◆ direction, e.g. local versus international

◆ destination, e.g. enclave versus nomadism

◆ impact, e.g. ecotourism versus purpose-built resort.

Quick check questions

1 What is a 'tourist enclave'?

2 Give two attractions of nomadic tourism.

3 What is meant by the term 'real income'?

4 Why might the volume of tourism fluctuate so much from one year to another?

5 Why does 'active tourism' usually have a bigger impact on an area than 'passive tourism'?

What is the relationship between the growth of tourism and economic development?

Student book pages 299–300

Key words

Disposable income   Invisible trade

Exchange rate

There is a positive correlation between the growth of tourism and economic development. As one increases so does the other but what is the cause and what is the effect?

If economic development increases (e.g. China) then there will be:

◆ more 'spare' or disposable wealth

◆ more leisure time – shorter working year/paid holidays

◆ improved transport, etc

◆ fewer political controls on travel

◆ more access to media

If tourism increases (e.g. Cuba) then there will be:

◆ increased foreign exchange earnings and foreign investment

◆ more employment – direct and indirect

◆ improved transport, etc

◆ greater exposure to alternative ideas and cultures

◆ growth of industries supplying tourists, e.g. farming, construction.

Case study: the UK and China

Student book pages 300–05

	UK – mature destination	China – new destination
Volume	2005 – 30m tourists in and 66m out	2005 – 25m tourists in and 31m out
Origin of visitors	USA, France, Germany, Ireland Increase within UK	South Korea, Japan, Russia Rapid increase within China
Type	Cultural, e.g. Shakespeare Historical, e.g. Tower of London Scenery, e.g. Scottish Highlands	Cultural, e.g. Forbidden City Historical, e.g. Great Wall Scenery, e.g. Yangtze
Spending	£32b on foreign holidays £85b from foreign visitors	£8b on foreign holidays £40b from foreign visitors
Impact	2m jobs 3.5% of UK economy	72m jobs 12% of China's economy
Future	Decrease in 'out' as economy falters Increase in 'in' as exchange rates favour Europe and from old 'colonial' LEDCs as they develop Growth of city holidays but decline of seaside holidays	Increase in both 'in' and 'out' as restrictions reduce and incomes rise Increase in 'in' as greater range of holiday destinations on offer, e.g. beach holidays and skiing Rapid growth of seaside holidays

Quick check questions

1 What is meant by the term 'exchange rate'?

2 Explain why the UK has a net benefit from tourism despite twice as many people going out for holidays as coming in.

3 What is the link between tourism and the improvement of transport?

4 What factor is the biggest drawback to holidaying in the UK?

5 Why is the number of tourists a) within and b) from outside increasing in China?

Social, economic and environmental issues with the growth of tourism

Student book pages 306–11

> **Exam tips**
>
> Remember that the impact of tourism is at both ends – origin and destination – and sometimes along the route as well.

Benefits and problems

(Think destination versus origin.)

Benefits

Physical:

◆ Encourages conservation, e.g. National Parks, historical sites

◆ Encourages control of pollution, dereliction, etc

◆ Encourages coastal and river protection

◆ Search for and development of new resources, e.g. water.

Economic:

◆ Creation of employment – easy to enter industry

◆ Increased investment in infrastructure – roads, power, etc

◆ Increased demand for local farm produce (move to cash farming)

◆ Demand for craft industries, shops, services, etc

◆ Earns foreign currency – balance of payments

◆ Can reduce rural to urban migration

◆ Can lead or focus development due to growth pole and multiplier effects.

Social:

◆ Improved education to meet needs of tourists

◆ Improved health services

◆ Traditional cultures preserved

◆ Development of foreign language skills

◆ Restrictive cultures made more liberal

◆ Introduces new ideas and expectations.

Political – opens up governments to new ideas

> **Exam tips**
>
> Remember Doxey's Model (Student book, page 307) suggests areas start off being enthusiastic about tourists but this evolves into irritation and then antagonism.

Problems

Physical:

◆ Construction destroys natural beauty/habitats

◆ Pollution – water, air, noise, litter, sewage

◆ Destruction of wildlife (disruption of breeding and wildlife taken as souvenirs)

◆ Water problems – loss of surface and groundwater (for swimming pools, golf courses, etc)

◆ Resource depletion, e.g. building materials, fuel

◆ Soil erosion, e.g. trampling.

Economic:

◆ Increased imports (cost) of food, etc

◆ Rise in prices, e.g. food, land

◆ Agriculture shifts to commercial so loss of stable food crops

◆ Most profits leave area (60–75 per cent)

◆ Loss of locally owned land

◆ Low-paid seasonal part-time and menial jobs

◆ Cost – takes money away from other areas/issues

◆ Huge drain on power and water supplies

◆ Urban coastal sprawl

◆ Traffic congestion

◆ Cost of infrastructure, e.g. roads, airport

◆ Economy over-dependent on tourism so vulnerable

◆ Increases foreign debt – high interest payments.

> **Key words**
>
> | | |
> |---|---|
> | Cost–benefit | Peripheral |
> | Cultural colonialism | Seasonal unemployment |
> | Growth pole | Spread |
> | Inequalities | Trickling down |
> | Multiplier | |

Social:

◆ Moral corruption – vice, crime, alcoholism, drugs

◆ Increased inequalities – 'them and us'

◆ Loss of traditional culture, language, values

◆ Cultural colonialism – spread of western culture, Macdonaldism

◆ Changed age structure as young move in to work in tourism

◆ Displacement of local population by tourist developments

◆ Loss of housing as tourists buy second homes.

Political – political unrest as new ideas threaten the 'status quo'.

Student book pages 312–15

> ### Exam tips
>
> Remember that tourism impacts on both the origin and destination, but also it impacts on the tourists themselves both positively and negatively.

	Jamaica – benefits	Myanmar – problems
	31% of GDP Employs 300,000	7% of GDP Employs 1.4m
Economic	Earns £2b a year Largest source of foreign exchange Greatly improved infrastructure, e.g. roads, power	Earnings spent on military Infrastructure patchy and developed around resorts
Environmental	Three National Parks created Entry fees pay for conservation Increasing eco-tourism Use of local suppliers for food, etc	Destruction of local habitats replaced by resorts, e.g. coastal mangroves, rainforest
Social	Sustainable Communities Foundation Through Tourism (SCF) programme is promoting community tourism where money filters down to local communities	1m displaced to beautify tourist areas Use of forced labour to clear areas Community structure destroyed
Political	Government set up a range of agencies to manage tourist development and make it more sustainable	Military dictatorship that has rushed to expand tourism but international boycott has limited expansion

The Butler model shows how tourism develops and changes over time.

> ### Remember
>
> Models are simplifications of reality and merely suggest logical patterns or trends. They are useful frameworks for answers.

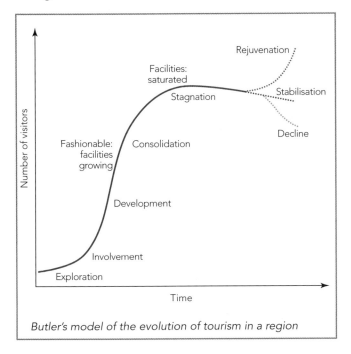

Butler's model of the evolution of tourism in a region

Quick check questions

1 Why are tourism earnings from international visitors counted as 'invisible trade'?

2 What are the problems associated with jobs in the tourist industry?

3 Why does tourism greatly increase the demand for water supplies?

4 Why might an increase in international tourism actually increase hunger in an LEDC?

5 Explain why tourism is so limited in Myanmar.

How can tourism be managed to ensure sustainability?

Student book pages 316–21

Sustainability is the ability to carry the system on into the future without a reduction in the system or standard of living.

Key words

Tourist hub	Ecological footprint
Honeypots	Carbon neutral
Conservation	

The threats to sustainability of tourism include:

- 'carbon footprint' of airplanes and other forms of transport
- destruction of ecosystems especially coastal, e.g. reefs
- overuse of local resources, e.g. water, energy
- cost of imported resources
- increased friction between visitors and locals
- westernisation of cultures
- variability in demand and often its seasonality.

Management challenges

Management challenges entail balancing the environmental needs (e.g. hydrology, vegetation) against economic needs (e.g. employment, tourist income, transport) and social needs (e.g. entertainment, historic/cultural aspects).

Key words

Tourist hubs	Slow travel
Destination footprint	Carbon offset

Managing tourism involves reducing inputs (e.g. energy, water, raw materials) and reducing harmful outputs (e.g. pollution) but also ensuring flows in the system are efficient (e.g. transport).

Issues:

- What is the exact nature of the environmental and water resources and their status (quality versus quantity)?
- Sheer cost – short versus long term, e.g. the damage tourism does to the environment. Who should pay? Local versus national issue – rate payer versus tax payer versus tourist. Some countries charge a tourist tax (e.g. Mexico).
- Who pays versus who gains? Should tax payers subsidise developments that benefit a small group of foreigners (e.g. tourists)? The construction of tourist enclaves (e.g. Cancun in Mexico) exemplifies this and the NIMBYism this produces. How effective is the scheme and for whom? What are the benefits and to whom?
- Political will – do local authorities or central government control schemes, e.g. golf courses in Scotland'?
- Technology – has the area the knowledge and expertise to develop the facilities or does it have to attract TNC investment, e.g. Cuba? Is enough known about that particular environment?
- Size or scale – definition of the area that makes up the project area. It is easier to manage smaller areas, e.g. a local beach compared to a coastline.
- How long will it take? Quick fix versus long term. Tourism is dynamic and fickle so developments can't be too long term in realisation, e.g. a single hotel complex is much quicker than an enclave.
- Wider impacts. What implications are there for areas beyond the project area? E.g. construction of Cancun hotel complexes had an impact along the Yucatan coast and for 80km inland.
- Can tourism ever be sustainable? If not, where can all those people go? Is it better to concentrate or spread the problems? Concentrations may be easier to deal with – honeypots.

Exam tips

Currently there are few attempts to regulate tourism and none on a global scale as most societies see the right to travel as one of their basic freedoms.

Approaches to sustainability

- Regulation, e.g. limit numbers (quotas) such as in the Grand Canyon National Park
- Planning and design, e.g. resorts in Mauritius are now planned to have the minimum impact on the environment
- Economic, e.g. charge or tax tourists (limits numbers and raises income to conserve, etc)
- Specialise, e.g. low volume but exclusive (high cost) tourism such as some Greek Islands
- Change the nature of tourism, e.g. fly less but stay longer.

Exam tips

You need to be able to contrast attempts at sustainable tourism. These ones are in terms of scale but it could be MEDC versus LEDC.

Case studies: sustainability

Student book pages 317–21

Scale	Example	Why it's sustainable
Local	El Pbutano, a farm in Ecuador Small scale – 16 guests stay in converted farmhouse made from local materials. Forest tours to learn about plants, etc. Small size group so little damage. Half of income goes to local community. Strict rules over interaction with local community	◆ Low numbers ◆ Limited activities – all in harmony with environment ◆ Strict controls over litter and waste ◆ Strict rules over contact with locals ◆ Strict rules over contact with plants and animals
Area	Peak District National Park As well as offering day-to-day guidance, the Authority is working with its partners to develop mid- to long-term plans and policies which will protect the National Park's landscape and wildlife while encouraging visitor access and sustaining its communities by developing the rural economy. It gets 22m visitors a year (65% for the day)	◆ Planning authority with brief to maintain character ◆ Has 109 conservation areas eligible for grants for restoration ◆ Series of community plans to manage impact of tourism ◆ Education service ◆ 15 habitat and seven species action plans to protect wildlife
Regional	Galapagos Islands, Ecuador Protects its image as a 'green destination'. All but 3% of the 13 islands are a national park. Limits tourist numbers and charges an entrance charge but illegal fishing and population growth threaten the sustainability	◆ Limits numbers of visitors including cruise ships and planes ◆ Uses the admission charges to fund conservation ◆ Has park rangers to patrol sensitive areas
Continental	Antarctica Voluntary code by tour operators. Currently there are few of these so operators can agree	◆ Numbers onshore are limited ◆ No accommodation onshore ◆ Most sensitive areas are avoided ◆ Must keep certain distance from wildlife ◆ Mustn't leave rubbish ◆ No collecting souvenirs ◆ Tourist ships controlled to ensure they have anti-pollution equipment

Ecotourism

A number of countries now see ecotourism as the answer as it involves low-volume and high-expenditure tourists who want to keep the environment they visit sustainable.

Costa Rica has:

◆ large areas of unspoilt rainforest with a wide range of wildlife

◆ created entirely new wildlife parks chiefly within the rainforest areas that have led to the construction of tourism facilities around them

◆ revenue retention arrangements that use earnings from entrance fees for wildlife park operations and conservation of natural habitats

◆ a policy to award contracts to local communities to operate food and souvenir concessions as a means of building local involvement in park conservation

◆ constructed nature trails, educational facilities and adventure activities with the overall aim of ecological sustainability and economic benefits to the local population

◆ a variable park entrance fee structure (charging higher fees to international tourists than to local visitors) to increase revenues.

Potential problems of ecotourism:

◆ Many countries see it as just nature-based tourism so ignore the sustainability and conservation elements

◆ Unregulated, ecotourism can still damage the environment and alter local cultures, e.g. pollution from rapid resort and hotel development around fragile park areas in Costa Rica

◆ Studies of ecotourism expenditures suggest that in most cases perhaps 20 to 30 per cent of the tourist expenditure stays in the national economy; even less reaches local communities.

◆ Ecotourism still introduces new elements into the natural environments – westernised hotels (albeit built with local materials), etc

◆ LEDCs fear that their parks and protected areas will become playgrounds for wealthy international tourists, with more land reserved for conservation and so less available for farming to feed and employ their expanding populations – could lead to increased imports.

So can tourism ever be fully sustainable? This may be possible in the sense that it can be made to pay for any disruption or damage it causes, but only if tourist numbers are drastically limited or reduced (such as by pricing). As global and national populations grow and wealth and expectations increase in more and more areas, so the pressure for more tourism will increase. It is seen as a natural right by many, but it brings tourists into direct conflict with the overall welfare of the planet (e.g. long-haul flights increasing global warming) and the welfare and sustainability of specific, often fragile, areas.

Quick check questions

1 What is meant by the term 'honeypot site'?

2 Why do you think there are no international agreements on tourism?

3 What is the main difference between National Parks in the UK and the USA?

4 How are the entrance fees charged to tourists used in Costa Rica?

5 What is the main problem with the income from ecotourism?

ExamCafé

Sample questions

1 (a) *Study Figure 4 which shows the seasonal pattern of tourist numbers to a Greek island (n.b. figure not included).*

i) Describe the pattern of tourist numbers shown in Figure 4. [4 marks]

◆ 'Pattern' here will probably be seasonal. To get to the higher level, remember to quote figures and months from the diagram in your answer.

ii) Suggest two reasons why the pattern shown in Figure 4 creates problems for the island. [6 marks]

◆ Remember this is linked to i) so if you have made an error in the first part you won't lose marks here provided you can give an answer appropriate to the pattern you identified.

◆ This question is looking for reasons for problems; not just the problems themselves:

Student Answer

The lack of winter tourists means that unemployment will rise as tourist activities will shut down until the spring. Also the lack of visitors in winter means that fewer boats and buses will run so transport around the island will become more difficult for the local population.

or:

Student Answer

The pattern shows that numbers of tourists differ greatly over the year. This means that there is excessive demand on tourist facilities such as accommodation, food, transport on the island. In winter there is excess capacity compared to tourist numbers so resources remain idle or close down increasing unemployment, etc.

◆ Clearly the second answer is more effective and operating at a higher level.

◆ Interestingly, you could argue that there are few problems created as the island adjusts to this rhythm because winter is its quiet time when there are no crops to harvest, etc.

(b) *Outline two economic opportunities created in an area by the growth of tourism. [6 marks]*

◆ This seems a very straightforward question but there are six marks at stake and simplistic answers such as 'creates more jobs' will not score highly. Detail is needed to get to the higher level – what type of job, for whom (most likely young females), where, etc. More perceptive candidates would anchor their answers to growth of tourism, not just tourism itself. A minor but subtle difference.

(c) *With reference to one or more examples, examine the environmental issues created by the growth of tourism. [9 marks]*

◆ Note that this question does not use the term 'problems' but uses 'issues' instead so some aspects might not be problems but opportunities. 'Environmental' normally suggests the physical environment – climate, relief, drainage, vegetation, habitats, pollution and soil but it can be interpreted as including human environmental issues. Be careful – do the physical first and if you have time/space then include human issues such as pollution.

Student Answer

Areas (1) undergoing the growth of tourism often experience water shortages (2) as tourists demand (3) large quantities for showers, drinking or for use in swimming pools (4).

◆ The part answer above is valid but needs improving to be fully effective:

(1) name an area, a real place such as Malaga in southern Spain
(2) where are the water shortages? It's often from reservoirs, lakes, rivers and from underground sources. It could also be put in context – southern Spain has a dry climate
(3) do they demand or is it more a case of 'expect'?
(4) one of the biggest uses of water is the watering of golf courses.

Essay questions

With reference to located examples, explain the recent growth in global tourism. [25 marks]

◆ Remember that 'recent' means the last 20 years but post-Second World War is acceptable. That could be crucial here as the reasons for the growth in the 60s and 70s (air transport, rise of the package holiday, etc) are different from those today and the growth is now occurring outside the MEDCs.

◆ Again, the issue is how to structure your answer – what should each paragraph contain that advances your overall argument? The most obvious structure is to look at the economic, social and political changes that have encouraged and enabled more people to travel for leisure. An alternative is to look at it historically or even by type of tourism – internal versus day trips versus international or by type of area – MEDC, LEDC, NIC.

◆ Growth in global tourism carries **two** meanings – sheer numbers in the world regardless of whether they are internal or international **and** the increase in those tourists travelling the globe as opposed to staying within their countries. Examiners will accept either or both.

◆ In this case the introduction is crucial in setting out what you understand from the wording of the question. You are also required to refer to located examples, which is not easy when this question is at a global scale. It is best to pick examples that illustrate some of the points you are making:

Student Answer

One reason is the increase in paid holidays and shorter working weeks. In the UK in 1970 the average worker had 2 weeks paid holiday but now it is 4 including bank holidays. This means there is double the opportunity to go away on holiday without any loss of income.

◆ This also illustrates the point that the use of logical, but possibly incorrect, figures is better than not using any at all.

Conclusion

Each chapter of this revision guide has given you an insight into the typical questions set on the topics both as short answer questions and longer essays but there is some final advice to be given. What you do at the very end when you enter that exam room can be critical, so the following Exam Café gives some advice for those final minutes.

Exam**Café**

In the Exam Room

Dos:

- Read the questions carefully – each word is crucial
- Understand what the command words are and what they mean
- Read **all** the question paper through first – your preference for an essay will influence your availability of choice in section A
- Remember in section A it's Coasts **or** Rivers and Cold **or** Hot arid, and in the human paper it's Urban **or** Rural and Energy **or** Tourism
- Remember in section A the questions for each topic get more difficult from part a) the most straight forward to d) the most complex
- Leave time to read through your essay to make sure it makes sense
- Answer your best question first – it should increase your confidence
- Answer the parts of your section A questions in order as one part may lead on to the next (NB parts i and ii are always linked)
- Use examples even if not specifically asked to, and examples should be clearly located
- Write clearly in the space provided as it will be scanned for marking
- Use diagrams and maps where **appropriate**
- Locate things carefully
- Spell geographical terms and places correctly, e.g. Mississippi.

Don'ts:

- Answer the essay from the same topic as your answers in section A
- Spend ten minutes on something worth four marks and five minutes on something worth nine marks
- Use colours on diagrams as they won't show up on scanning
- Cross out work you think is wrong (until the end).

Finally

- Above all, read the question carefully noting the key aspects and terms, and then answer it covering all these aspects, not giving the answer to the question you hoped would come up.

Answers to quick check questions

Chapter 1 River environments

Processes at work in river basins

1. 9%.
2. Chemical.
3. Mechanical.
4. a) free fall, avalanche, flow, slide, creep
   b) dry – creep, free fall, avalanche, slide, flow.
5. The slope that is at rest – in equilibrium with the conditions so unlikely to move.

Factors responsible for fluvial processes and landforms

1. Channel a: a) 3.6 (125/35) b) 7 (5/7).7
2. Rivers can not flow below this or they would have to flow uphill.
3. Lake.
4. Soil, groundwater, lakes, vegetation, snow.
5. a) machinery compacts soil, crops in rows, removal of trees, irrigation. b) plant tree/bush crops, contour plough, harrow soil.

River features

1. They erode on the faster outside of the bend and deposit a slip-off slope on the slower moving inside of the bend.
2. They erode the outside and deposit on the inside so shifting the channel.
3. A hard rock type with a weakness and eddying or turbulent flow (or load with which to erode).
4. They enable the river to be above the surrounding land so if they break they cause floods.
5. They require very still coastal water – no tides or currents.

Flooding

1. August, due to heavy convectional storms.
2. UK is away from a plate margin.
3. 50% is below 5m and the area is a delta and slowly sinking.
4. Lack of funds (priorities are elsewhere).
5. Hard involves major large-scale construction unlike soft that uses natural defences, e.g. tree planting.

Chapter 2 Coastal environments

Coastal processes

1. Lack of vegetation to bind the rock due to salt and continual trigger of eroding waves.
2. They have vast wind energy that is converted into strong wave energy and coasts are more open to storms (less friction from the sea slowing them).
3. Rising sea level so more wave energy as deeper water due to post-glacial rise in sea level.
4. Geology of beach material – if not local then unlikely to be longshore in origin.
5. Opens up coast to erosion as mangrove used to absorb wave energy and mangrove used to collect silt so increases coastal deposition.

Factors responsible for coastal processes and landforms

1. It is the length over which the wind can operate so controls how much energy the waves can absorb – long fetch = a lot of energy.
2. Constructive – as backwash is weak and there is less energy in the wave.
3. Depends on the rock type and structure but generally discordant (end on to the waves) is the more easily eroded.
4. Lagoons, saltmarshes.
5. It forms a beach.

How coasts can be protected

1. Softness of the bedrock – unconsolidated till.
2. It would cost too much and not a consistently high population density or economic importance.
3. They do not look pleasant and it makes access to the beach difficult.
4. Mainly with tourists who want beach access. Can lead to fires and tourists trample the vegetation. Also conservationists who want to see 'natural vegetation'.
5. Loss of productive and fertile farmland – especially with rising food prices and shortages, it took a long time to reclaim the land so it is a loss of investment or it allows the sea further inland.

Management challenges associated with coastal development

1. They indicate where impacts of a scheme designed for one area may also occur – it is a feedback loop and should not be ignored.
2. No – they lack the finances to pay for effective but expensive defences.
3. Via control of planning permission for any developments.
4. Department for the Environment, Farming and Rural Affairs.
5. How do you put figures on people's feelings, homes etc? How are local issues balanced with regional issues? Who pays and who benefits?

Chapter 3 Cold environments

Processes at work in cold environments

1. Because snow is much lower density than rain so a small level of precipitation can result in large snowfalls and snow drifts in the strong winds.
2. No – solution by carbonic acid actually speeds up.
3. Scratches (striations) on bare rock and polishing of rocks.
4. A film of water at their base allows them to skid quickly with little down pressure on the bedrock.
5. Glacial is unbedded and unsorted unlike fluvio-glacial deposits.

Features of cold areas

1. Hanging valleys, truncated spurs, waterfalls, lateral moraines, lakes (or old lake floors).
2. Too warm for snow/ice to remain over the year.
3. A small lake usually in a cirque or corrie.
4. One steeper side (the ice contact face).
5. Often farming and vegetation has obscured the deposits.

Why so fragile?

1. Less prone to frost damage (stay protected under the snow) and need less nutrients.
2. Needle leaves, cone bearing, evergreen, anti-freeze in thickly barked trunks.
3. Soil – soil is waterlogged or frozen and very acid so few nutrients available.
4. They hibernate or migrate in winter.
5. Ecosystem is designed for resisting cold so it quickly breaks down if no cold phase occurs.

How can cold areas be managed sustainably?

1. Oil and gas discoveries (world energy shortage).
2. It was always too hostile, remote and expensive – now these are seen as attractions.
3. Search for minerals especially fossil fuels.
4. Built on stilts or on insulating layers.
5. The Alps cover parts of eight countries – they all had to agree as many aspects cross borders.

Chapter 4 Hot arid and semi-arid environments

Processes at work in hot arid environments

1. Atmospheric air circulation that produces descending air at the tropics.
2. Clear skies allow rapid radiation cooling.
3. Great differences in pressure and little to slow the wind – little vegetation.
4. With the particles it carries.
5. A river 'born' outside the arid area but large enough to flow through it.

Features of hot arid areas

1. Thunderstorms with rain hitting baked hard impervious ground so runoff is rapid.
2. Flash floods miles away can rush down a wadi with little warning.
3. Evaporation of lake water that is high in salt leaves the salt behind as it crystalises out.
4. No. Much is rock – sand will get blown away easily and collect in areas such as 'sand seas'.
5. Heaviest most erosive particles are carried at the base of the wind column.

Why so fragile?

1. To reduce water loss.
2. To maximise heat loss (ears have lots of blood vessels) and sound travels in deserts so good hearing is a defence mechanism.
3. When it rains the seeds and plants in the desert are triggered into rapid life cycles including flowering.
4. Cooler at night and less water loss and safer.
5. Reliable sunny, dry climate.

How can hot arid areas be managed sustainably?

1. Salinisation due to high evaporation rate.
2. The powers (often colonial) that set them up considered the desert a waste land with few distinctive features. This always has caused problems as they divide nomadic grazing lands and mineral deposits.
3. International borders are difficult to cross and few young want to continue the lifestyle.
4. Massive demand for water.
5. Low cost and build on local population's expertise.

Chapter 5 Managing urban change

Factors that influence land-use patterns

1. Uniform physical area, bid-rent, family status or life cycle, pre-industrial urban area.
2. Counterurbanisation.

3. More wealthy population moving into an area so upgrading it.
4. Land transport was poor, slow and often dangerous.
5. Make it more central to the country, show its independence, start again in a planned way.

Urban change – causes/issues
1. It is relative to the levels of income or wealth.
2. It is where people are excluded from financial institutions such as banks by their location and its reputation.
3. Property prices.
4. More wealthy (so pay more tax) are moving out of urban areas.
5. Assisted Self Help.

Environmental issues
1. Greater incomes or wealth – seen as status symbol.
2. a) limited sites, methane and groundwater pollution b) produces cancer-producing dioxins.
3. Traffic fumes (especially ozone) reacting with sunlight.
4. Increased mobility – greater car ownership.
5. It creates more impervious surfaces so runoff increases and infiltration decreases.

How can urban areas be managed sustainably?
1. Not In My Back Yard.
2. 125 times its surface area.
3. Sewage is used to produce bio-gas that is then used as a fuel for heating or powering vehicles.
4. A town that is carbon neutral in its construction and operation.
5. It is in the delta of a major river and could be vulnerable to a rising sea level.

Chapter 6 Managing rural change

Factors that influence the opportunities and development of rural areas
1. Intensive farming has a high input to a small area ratio to produce a high yield. Extensive farming is the reverse.
2. Arable farming has more fixed investments such as specialised equipment, field layout and crops in the ground. Pastoral farming: it is relatively easy to move the animals in a short time.
3. Constant heat and precipitation result in an all-year-round yield for tree crops, which is important to supply the processing plants.
4. Improved transport and desire for village life style.
5. Migrant workers.

Rural change – causes/issues
1. Migration into urban areas (and famines, wars, etc, increasing the rural death rate).

2. Forces up house prices (equally causes villages to 'die' – lose services, etc).
3. Retirement influx and the young move to urban areas for the 'bright lights'.
4. Decreased birth rate as young move to urban areas.
5. Improvement in communications so more can migrate out of the area.

Environmental issues
1. Fertilisers get into lakes, etc, and algae expand using the nutrients. They extract oxygen and block the light from the lower layers so lake life dies.
2. Narrow windy roads with numerous bottlenecks not designed for modern traffic.
3. Common Agricultural Policy.
4. It can wash out minerals from the soil and waterlog it. In hot areas, evaporation causes salts to build up and kill crops.
5. It is more open to pests, disease and the weather.

How can urban areas be managed sustainably?
1. Increasing food shortages and rising prices.
2. Recreation and tourism.
3. Site of Special Scientific Interest.
4. By planning regulations and controls.
5. Problems and pressures are not limited by borders and problems tend to be on a larger scale than in the past (e.g. pollution); and a way of gaining more help/resources.

Chapter 7 The energy issue

Availability of energy – global patterns
1. If you cut it faster than it can grow, you will kill it and so it stops being renewable.
2. Middle East.
3. It was a nuclear disaster that highlighted the dangers of nuclear power stations so few countries pursued a nuclear programme after that event.
4. UK oil is low in sulphur so is valuable; the UK needs cheaper heavy oil for by-products such as plastics, etc.
5. Firewood – leads to deforestation and desertification.

The issues associated with a rising demand for energy
1. It's only one source of greenhouse gases and there is already so much greenhouse gas in the upper atmosphere that the effect is unlikely to be slowed.
2. It produces very little fuel itself yet has a massive demand for energy.

3. Most of its energy comes from hydro-electricity so little oil is needed.
4. Corruption and TNCs control the industry.
5. It is the TNCs that have the expertise, capital and technology to develop energy resources.

Managing energy to ensure sustainability

1. There is a finite amount of these minerals.
2. Price.
3. Variability of the wind (also unsightliness and noise).
4. One of the largest tidal ranges in the world.
5. They supply 'green' energy but they take up land that was used for food crops and often they need more energy to grow them than they produce.

Chapter 8 The growth of tourism

Reasons for growth

1. An area set aside exclusively for tourism usually with little contact with the surrounding area.
2. Variety and ever-changing scenery.
3. What the income is worth in terms of what it can purchase.
4. Tourists respond to political problems, economic changes, weather, disasters and the like both at the destination and their origin. Tourists have a lot of choices as alternatives.
5. Active, unlike passive, usually requires equipment or special facilities, e.g. skiing.

What is the relationship between the growth of tourism and economic development?

1. The rate at which one currency can purchase another.
2. Foreign visitors spend more in the UK than UK visitors spend abroad.
3. Tourist need good airports/ports to arrive and depart from and want good roads to get around on to see the sights, etc.
4. The weather.
5. a) increasing affluence and more freedom to travel b) increasing incomes and a desire to visit more distant and exotic cultures.

Social, economic and environmental issues with the growth of tourism

1. It is a service. No visible item exchanges hands.
2. They are often low paid, seasonal and menial.
3. Tourists expect swimming pools, showers, etc.
4. Land is taken up to grow crops to supply hotels or farmland is built on so less staple food crops are produced and prices rise.
5. Political unrest and controls put visitors off.

How can tourism be managed to ensure sustainability?

1. A site that is designed to attract a lot of visitors (often away from other areas).
2. Travel is seen as a basic human right and freedom. There is a lot of competition to attract tourists so countries are unlikely to agree on any controls.
3. In the USA they are state owned but in private ownership in the UK.
4. Used for conservation and protection for the environment.
5. Most of it leaves the area or country.